ANDY MERRIFIELD is an independent scholar and author of a dozen books, as well as numerous articles, essays and reviews appearing in *Monthly Review*, *The Nation*, *Harper's Magazine*, *New Left Review*, *The Guardian*, *Literary Hub*, *Jacobin*, and *Dissent*. He is a prolific writer about urbanism, political theory, and literature. His books include *Dialectical Urbanism* (Monthly Review Press), *The New Urban Question*, and *Magical Marxism*. He has also published three intellectual biographies, of Henri Lefebvre, Guy Debord, and John Berger, a popular existential travelogue, *The Wisdom of Donkeys*, a manifesto for liberated living, *The Amateur*, together with a memoir about cities and love, inspired by Raymond Carver's short stories, called *What We Talk About When We Talk About Cities (and Love)*.

MARX
DEAD AND ALIVE
Reading Capital in Precarious Times

ANDY MERRIFIELD

MONTHLY REVIEW PRESS

New York

Library of Congress Cataloging-in-Publication Data:
Merrifield, Andy, author.
Marx, dead and alive : reading Capital in precarious times / Andy
    Merrifield.
Identifiers: LCCN 2020031943 | ISBN 9781583678794
(paperback) | ISBN   9781583678800 (cloth) | ISBN
9781583678817 (ebook) | ISBN 9781583678824 (ebook other)
Subjects: LCSH: Marx, Karl, 1818-1883. | Marx, Karl, 1818-
1883. Kapital. | Capitalism. | Socialism.
Classification: LCC HX39.5 .M457 2020 | DDC 335.4--dc23
LC record available at https://lccn.loc.gov/2020031943

Typeset in Bulmer

MONTHLY REVIEW PRESS, NEW YORK
monthlyreview.org
5 4 3 2 1

Marx, Dead and Alive

1.

At a quarter to three in the afternoon, March 14, 1883, Karl Marx passed away peacefully in his favorite armchair. Three days later, a few miles up the road, he was buried, a citizenless émigré, in London's Highgate Cemetery. At the graveside, eleven mourners paid homage to "Old Moor," and listened to Marx's longtime comrade and benefactor, Frederick Engels, "The General," remember his dear departed friend: "An immeasurable loss has been sustained both by the militant proletariat of Europe and America, and by historical science, in the death of this man. The gap that has been left by the departure of this mighty spirit will soon enough make itself felt." "His name," Engels predicted, "will endure through the ages, and so also will his thought."

One hundred and thirty-six years on, Highgate Cemetery continues to receive a steady stream of Marx well-wishers, of all ages and nationalities, the curious and the converted. Fresh flowers and moving inscriptions, in almost every language under the sun, regularly adorn the great revolutionary's gravestone. Towering overhead, seemingly indomitable, is the man himself, or rather a gigantic bust of him, with its menacing eyes staring out into the distance, perhaps frowning at his conservative rival Herbert Spencer, whose remains lie opposite across the path.

Over the years, the cemetery has attracted its fair share of naysayers as well, people who have it in for Marx and all he stands for. Reactionaries have taken hammers and chisels to his monument, daubed graffiti over it, and, in a 1970 National Front attack, tried to blow it up with a pipe bomb. But the grave's design—solid bronze bust with a Cornish granite plinth—has so far resisted everything thrown at it. I say "so far" because just this past week, as I write—late February 2019—perhaps the nastiest attack to date has been perpetrated; the Grade I-listed monument might never be the same again. The nastiest attack in the nastiest of times, and that, alas, is no coincidence.

In early February, vandals took a blunt instrument to Marx's headstone. But they hadn't reckoned on its thickness. So they returned later that same night, with what seems like a lump hammer, taking further swipes. This time they shattered pieces from the tablet, those bearing the letters of Marx's name, as well as members of his family, including his four-year-old grandson, Harry Longuet. And then, several weeks on, the tomb was ransacked a second time, splattered with lurid red paint, saying: "Doctrine of Hate" and "Architect of Genocide." Ian Dungavell, Chief Executive of Friends of Highgate Cemetery Trust, a man responsible for the cemetery's 53,000 graves, was shocked by both assaults, condemning them as a "particularly inarticulate form of political comment."

My heart sank when I heard the news. Perhaps because I knew that, these days, inarticulacy is very much the form of our political commentary. Maybe, too, because over past decades I've tried to articulate my own vision of Marx and Marxism. Marx's thought has never been rigid dogma or some sterile formula for me. Instead, it's a rich source of ideas, a vibrant critical (and self-critical) culture capable of innumerable spin-offs and reinterpretations, imaginative adaptations, and provocations. Marx's vision is about human liberation, not collective enslavement. Why would any tyrant ever imagine a society in which "the free development of each is the condition for the free development of all"?

Marx's thought has survived for more than a century and a half because of this fluidity and dynamism. Marxism has given people plenty to work with and think about when the world itself has been less inspiring. A while back, the late Eduardo Galeano advocated a Marxism that "celebrates continuous birth." He had one of his rummy characters call it *Magical Marxism*: "one half reason, one half passion, and a third half mystery." "Not a bad idea!" his drinking buddies agree, toasting this new school of Marxism, which has always seemed like a good idea to me, too, even if I'd fill that third half with *hope*.

I say all this without being smitten by Marx's Highgate bust—by an immense, iconic image of the man, and of Marxism, a Marxism of big statues and flag-waving, of a holy orthodoxy far removed from the messy profane world of real mortals. Marx himself, of course, occupied this messy profane world. In real life, he was an intricate and vulnerable figure, a feisty yet frail patriarch, a poor, peripatetic vagabond who spent more than thirty years traipsing from one crummy London apartment to another, his whole family often living in just two cluttered rooms, avoiding debts, pawning what little he had (including his own overcoat), shrugging off illness, watching four children predecease him.

Marx's personal pains far exceeded his political woes. Never had anyone, he once said of himself, written about capital in general amid a total lack of capital in particular. Marx's own ironic Marxism often seemed more akin to a Groucho Marxism, avoiding any club that would have *him* as a member: "I, at least, am not a Marxist," he is once reputed to have a told a French socialist, after seeing his thought bastardized. More often than not Marx resembled a disheveled character from Dostoevsky or Gogol, having his overcoat ripped off his back, feeling the chill breeze of the economy and the climate pierce his threadbare clothing. The *Communist Manifesto* is full of such imagery.

Marx's clumsy outsiderness, his foreignness, his broken English, could have easily earned him a lead role in a Samuel Beckett performance. Marx knew the dingy bedsit tenancies populated by the likes of Murphy, or the anonymous evictee of "The Expelled," flung out onto the rooming-house's steps, hearing the door slam behind him. Marx's alter-egos were more Watt than Stalin, more Molloy than Mao. His Vladimir was a Didi not an Ilyich. He was the intellectual champion of the underdog principally because he was one. He learned about the brutality of capitalism from political activism and mammoth reading sessions in the British Museum; yet his knowledge of working-class domestic oppression came firsthand, was lived out. A prophet of genocide? Give me a break.

I was beginning to agree with the Marxist academic Fredric Jameson that it's easier to imagine the end of the world than the end of capitalism. Some days, it does feel like we are living through the end of the world. Everything seems such a hopeless dead-end—our politics and economy, our high-tech culture, our collective future. Maybe it's a sort of an endgame: the game is up yet somehow the match goes on, square by square, pawns beside kings. "It's time it ended," Hamm says in *Endgame*, Beckett's play about the end of the world, a world that had ended yet continues to trudge on miserably. "Clov," Hamm asks his half-crippled assistant, in a question we might pose today, if only to ourselves, "Have you had enough?" "Yes!" Clov answers. Then, pausing, wonders, "Of what?" "Of this . . . this . . . thing," says Hamm. "I always had," says Clov.

Have you had enough? Of what? Of this . . . this . . . thing? At low times, I've really had enough. I suspect I'm not the only one. Daily with the news: I try to avoid looking, try to close my ears. Yet I hear it everywhere. Newspapers. People talking. On screens. In the air. This thing that depresses. Trump? Brexit? Climate meltdown? Consumer capitalism? And then the desecration of Marx's grave, which tipped me over the edge, or else brought on a raging fever. (All this had been written before the coronavirus.) I knew then how Wallace Shawn's protagonist felt in *The Fever*, a play about a contagion that's really a political reawakening.[1] "Outside of here it's death," says Hamm, of another contagion. "Beyond is the other hell."

Looking through his spyglass, at the outside, Clov says, "Nothing stirs. All is—" "All is what?" demands Hamm. "What all is? in a word? Corpsed," says Clov.

Our own corpsed reality has depressed me so much that I vowed now was the time to get back to Marx. It had been a while since I'd read him closely, and twenty years since I'd taught him at university, in my former academic days in America. Thus my pledge to get back to Marx, back to *Capital*, back to his thought, really reading it again, closely. I know it might sound pretentious to say *re*read Marx, but that would be truer, since I must have read Volume One of *Capital*, first published in German in 1867, a half-dozen times, at least. I remember the first time I'd read it, in 1986, during Thatcher's second term, in what is now a tatty Penguin edition (originally published in 1976). Those old annotations I can see have to make way for new scribbles and underlinings, appropriate to our current conjuncture. Marx spoke to me in dark times in the 1980s and he can still speak to us in the even darker times now.

I thought this as I walked up the hill of Swain's Lane, on my way to Highgate Cemetery, to its East Wing, going to pay homage to Old Moor myself, to see what was happening to his vandalized grave. The brutality of the attack shocked me. Some of the red paint had already been scrubbed off. Yet the granite plinth had been assaulted with terrifying force, by someone verging on the demented. Scary that they're still walking London's streets. I took a photo of the damage, along with the little bunch of daffodils some gentle soul had placed there.

One suspects that the perpetrator was himself an underdog, someone who feels a bilious rage inside, enough to lash out rightward. There are a lot of bouquets at the base of the grave, from all over the globe, and a sign, on A4 paper, taped on the plinth, left by a Turkish Revolutionary Path member. Torn but intact, it reads, in red uppercase: "YOU CAN DESTROY MARX'S GRAVESTONE, BUT YOU CANNOT DESTROY HIS IDEOLOGY." "Normally," said Ian Dungavell, "we take signs down, but on this occasion, I think we'll leave it."[2] It's a nice thought: that

that ideology, that those ideas, might still be blowing in the wind, alive and kicking, despite the hammer blows raining down on them, trying to destroy them.

2.

Marx can help us through these dark times. He can help us journey through them, not around them. In what follows, I want to take readers into Marx's *Capital*, into Marx himself, the person; to get analytical with him, follow his thought process, cut through the nonsense of his times, together with the nonsense of ours. I also want to laugh with him—he's one of great comic writers, after all, the master of the sardonic put-down, the brilliant castigator of the moron and the charlatan. There's a lot a steady work still to do there.

Marx's subject matter was highly dynamic capitalist society, constantly changing, forever in flux, complex and contradictory. At the British Museum, he was an avid reader of *The Economist*. Each week he had at hand new information that he'd interrogate, news from Russia and the United States, news of new cycles of industrial development and class wars over the working day in England, which *The Economist* invariably scorned. It was all grist to Marx's critical mill. The information flow never seemed to end. How, then, could his analysis ever stop? So it goes. But no, nothing just went for Marx. Nothing ever happens naturally, is ever self-evident for him. There were always forces creating, mutually conspiring, undermining each other, upending one another, always reasons and explanations for why this and not that; and Marx wanted to explain all, to know all, to leave nothing out. How could *Capital* end so long as capital went on accumulating, went on transforming the world? His monomania expressed the madness of the subject, not of the author.

Marx never wanted to finish *Capital* because he couldn't see how it could ever be finished. He sought the definitive but knew the impossibility of the definitive. It tormented him. Yet, ironically, the fact that he never finished *Capital*, in all its three volumes, only ever taking Volume One to the printer's shop, is our blessing, our opportunity. We can update his work, explore the layer upon layer of Marx's paint, and do our own touching up along the way. In so doing we can visualize his canvas not just as a portrayal of Dickensian hard times but as an image of modern times as well, of hopes and visions for a culture forever changeable and always up for grabs. Then we might recognize Marx's narrative as *our* narrative—*de te fabula narratur*, as he says. a tale about us, necessary for his epoch, indispensable for our own.

NOT LONG AFTER I STARTED TO READ *Capital* again, I was traveling on a train back from London's Gatwick Airport, sitting next to the window, calmly leafing through Volume One. It was early days in my rereading and it was likely chapter 1, on the commodity, that preoccupied me. Suddenly, just as the train was about to depart, an immaculately dressed West African man sat down beside me and after a while began reading a similarly thick tome. I looked over and saw him, very attentively, almost lovingly, poring over the Bible. There were many passages underscored in pencil. I'd underscored many passages of my *Capital* in pencil. Here was I, with *Capital*, and him, with the Bible, two people gripped by two big books, roughly the same size, that pretty much covered the bases of Western civilization, just as, all around us, everybody else twiddled pitifully on their cell phones.

Never in my life have I taken *Capital* as a sacred text, to be read as an act of faith, with the absolute belief that, one day, the communist messiah would arrive. In Marx's secular imagination, everything holy became profane. To read his work as a sort of catechism, without doubts or disagreement, I've always thought problematic. And yet, there's a sense in which I'd change my tune a bit now. Not out of any religious epiphany; more because Marx's *Capital* is a text, like the Bible, that can help readers attribute meaning to their lives; they can use it, study it, live it out, pore over it, as a guiding spirit. Underscore passages in pencil if they want, too. Whatever the case, reading *Capital* can be a nourishing experience. I hope this book might pique people's curiosity to make them want to discover this nourishing experience for themselves.

Marx is important today not necessarily because he was right, as Terry Eagleton has argued;[3] but because he matters even if he was wrong. Anyway, it's probably too early to tell whether he was right or not wrong. Marx, instead, challenges us, like God challenged Job, tests us out, tries to get us to live up to the promise and possibility of what he laid before us, of what he saw resided inside us. Marx knew there was something absurd about the reality we had created for ourselves. We can do better—a whole lot better.

One of the more contentious ideas in the Marxist tradition, something Marx himself only hinted at, is *false consciousness*. Here it's important to draw attention to *ideology*, to Marx's own special notion of what it constitutes. Ideology, for him, is information transmitting an *implicit* message. In fact, this message doesn't seem like it's a message at all, doesn't appear like it's communicating something hidden, something *unstated*; at first blush it seems plausible, and first blush is often enough for it to be believed. Each time we read the *Daily Mail*, or listen to commercial radio and news channels, we are reading and listening to ideology.

These mouthpieces are at best the purveyors of partial truths. They tell us what they want us to know, nothing more, usually a lot less. Often what they tell us is deliberate misinformation, pure unadulterated lies. They conspire to provide people with an implicitly distorted sense of reality, one beneficial to vested political and economic interests. But they are believed by vast audiences. So these falsities become real, get embedded in people's brains. These days, it's nothing short of a form of brainwashing, such is the ubiquity of mass (and social) media invading people's lives. "The people," in a nutshell, have been hauled in, hook, line, and sinker, into believing a reality that is false, that is frequently counter to their best interests. Hence *false consciousness*.

The peddlers of ideology, meanwhile, have another string in their bow. They're able to dismiss critical knowledge, like Marx's, as ideological because it has an *explicit* political message—which, if you think about it, is always easier to dismiss. Marx conceived a body of thought and set of ideas—an ideology, if you will—that is openly honest about where it is coming from, as a mode of thinking that explicitly tries to frame things from the standpoint of ordinary working-class people. This is how capitalist society appears, Marx says, how it operates if you view it from the perspective of a worker—not from the perspective of the greedy boss or parasitic landlord, nor from the Etonian public schoolboy or billionaire hedge-funder.

Still, in saying this, what endures about the analysis in *Capital* is Marx's rigor, his intellectual honesty, his desire to tell it how it really is, yet to tell it *fairly*, within the rules of legitimate knowledge. Not make-believe, not deliberate deceit. He leaves us with a body of thought, as well as a methodology, that can challenge these deeply troubling "post-truth" times of ours, that can stand up to them, puncture the ideological illusions enveloping everything we hear, everything we do, everything we have become.

3.

Everybody says, even Marx himself, that those early chapters of *Capital* are the most difficult. In 1872, Marx was thrilled to see his great work translated into French and serialized. But he warned French readers not to be too hasty: "The method of analysis which I employed," he said, "and which had not previously been applied to economic subjects, makes the reading of the first chapters rather arduous." He feared that "the French public, always impatient to come to a conclusion, eager to know the connection between general principles and the immediate questions that have aroused their passions, may be disheartened because they will be unable to move on at once."

But despite Marx's cautioning, there's something wonderfully dizzying about moving with his thought process, hearing his often poetic lyricism, and following his analytical logic, even getting bogged down in it. What Marx is up to early on in *Capital* is something today we might call *coding*. He is programming capitalism, and reading him is our attempt to download the critical app he's created for us, the conceptual software that allows us, step by step, contradiction by contradiction, to trace out capitalism's whole evolutionary movement, its value hieroglyphic.

Marx's plane of immanence incorporates the whole wide capitalist world, with its intricate web of global money flows and commodity exchanges, of capital accumulating and stock prices rising and dipping. This system taps into the furthest and widest reaches of our planet while plumbing the depths of our everyday lives. And yet, for all that, its atomic composition, its basic constitutive part—its "cell-form," Marx calls it—is the "ostensibly trivial" commodity, abounding in all sorts of "metaphysical subtleties and theological niceties." What Marx wants to demonstrate here is how such "a motley mosaic of disparate and unconnected expressions of value" aren't so disparate and unconnected as we might think.

One of the great cameo appearances in chapter 1 of *Capital* is the tailor, together with his trusty product, the coat. For a dozen or more pages, the tailor's coat, and its counterpart, the linen, are the subject of some of the weirdest and most brilliant dialectical sections of Marx's whole text. Marx is being serious, we know, sometimes deadly serious. But there's wit here, too, and I think Marx knows he's playing with us a little. For centuries, he says, humans have made coats without a single person ever becoming a tailor. It's only with the advent of capitalism that tailoring became a specialist trade, "an independent branch of the social division of labour." Suddenly, the tailor's wares became value-creating abstract labour, the coat an objectification, the incarnation of "socially necessary labour time," a material thing extinguished of all sensuous characteristics, exchanged on the marketplace for money.

This is how Marx puts it:

> In the production of the coat, human labour-power, in the shape of tailoring, has in actual fact been expended. Human labour has therefore been accumulated in the coat. From this point of view, the coat is a 'bearer of value,' although this property never shows through, even when the coat is at its most threadbare. In its value-relation with the linen, the coat counts only under this aspect, counts therefore as embodied value, as the body of value. Despite its buttoned up appearance, the linen recognizes in it a splendid kindred soul, the soul of value.

"As a use-value," Marx continues,

> the linen is something palpably different from the coat; as value, it is identical with the coat and therefore looks like the coat. Thus the linen acquires a value-form

different from its natural form. Its existence as value is manifested in its equality with the coat, just as the sheep-like nature of the Christian is shown in his re-semblance to the Lamb of God.

"In order to inform us that the linen's sublime objec-tivity as a value," Marx says a bit later, "differs from its stiff and starchy existence as a body, it says that value has the appearance of a coat, and therefore that in so far as the linen itself is an object of value, it and the coat are as alike as two peas."

And again:

In the value-relation of commodity A to commodity B, of the linen to the coat, not only is the commodity-type coat equated with the linen in qualitative terms as an object of value as such, but also a definite quantity of the object of value or equivalent; 1 coat, for example, is equated with a definite quantity of linen, such as 20 yards. The equation 20 yards of linen = 1 coat, or 20 yards of linen are worth 1 coat, presupposes the pres-ence in 1 coat of exactly as much or the substance of value as there is in 20 yards of linen, implies therefore that the quantities in which the two commodities are present have the cost of the same amount of labour or the same quantity of labour-power.

And a few pages on, Marx resumes:

If one kind of commodity, such as a coat, serves as the equivalent of another, such as linen, and coats therefore acquire the characteristic property of being in a form in which they can be directly exchanged with the linen, this still by no means provides us with the proportion in which the two are exchangeable. Since the magnitude of the value of the linen is a given quantity, this proportion depends on the magnitude of the coat's value. Whether the coat is expressed as the equivalent and the linen as relative value, or, inversely, the linen is expressed as equivalent and the coat as relative value, the magnitude of the coat's value is determined, as ever, by the labour-time necessary for its production, independently of its value-form. But as soon as the coat takes up the position of the equivalent in the value expression, the magnitude of its value ceases to be expressed quantitatively.

Thus "the relative value-form of a commodity," Marx says, "the linen for example,

expresses its value-existence as something wholly different from its substance and properties, as the quality of being comparable with a coat for example; this expression itself therefore indicates it conceals a social relation. . . . The coat, therefore, seems to be endowed with its equivalent form, its property of direct exchange ability, by nature, just as much as its property of being heavy or its ability to keep us warm. Hence the mysteriousness of the equivalent form, which only impinges on the crude bourgeois vision of the political economist when it confronts him in its fully developed shape, that of money.

WHEN I READ THESE ZANY SECTIONS on the coat, I had not long ago finished Samuel Beckett's early novel *Watt*, written in the south of France in the early 1940s, as the author fled Nazi occupation. What struck me immediately were the similarities between both men's mode of argumentation, their irresistible urge to understand inexplicable realities through dialectical gyrations. At Knott's house, Watt fixates on the pot much as Marx had fixated on the coat.

"Watt was greatly troubled by this tiny little thing," says Beckett,

> more troubled perhaps than he had ever been by anything, and Watt had been frequently and exceedingly troubled, in his time, by this imperceptible, no, hardly imperceptible, since he perceived it, by this undefinable thing that prevented him from saying of the object that was so like a pot, that it was a pot, and of the creature that still in spite of everything presented a large number of exclusively human characteristics, that it was a man. Thus of the pseudo-pot he would say, after reflection, It is a shield, or, growing bolder, It is a raven, and so on. But the pot proved as little a shield, or a raven, or any other of the things that Watt called it, as a pot.

Yet Watt's logic is much less politically charged than Marx's. The coat, for Marx, has profound political as well as dialectical significance. We might even say that the political significance of the coat emanated from the personal significance of the coat. Peter Stallybrass's essay, "Marx's Coat," offers a fascinating glimpse of poor Marx, not only journeying to the British Museum in his old overcoat, but also periodically to the pawnbroker with it as well.[4] Marx was so broke that he was often forced to sell what little he had. One time, he went to the pawnbroker with wife Jenny's family silver, a precious heirloom. He was unkempt, with a ragged mane, and the silver bore the crest of the Duke of Argyll. The pawnbroker, seeing such a noble stamp peddled by such a wretched soul, became suspicious and called the cops, who took Marx away to the station, locking him up in a cell for the night.

Throughout the 1850s and 1860s, Marx's coat was in and out of the pawnshop. When Marx's fortunes perked up—if either he'd published a piece of paid journalism in the *New York Daily Tribune*, or Engels helped out—he'd go back to the pawnbroker and try to redeem his old coat. Until then, he'd be housebound, especially in winter. Without his coat, no British Museum. Without the British Museum, no research for *Capital*. "What clothes Marx wore," Stallybrass says, "thus shaped what he wrote." As a use-value, Marx's coat kept him warm in winter and brought him the appearance of a respectable gent, able to access the bourgeois Reading Room of the British Museum. But as an exchange-value, his coat is evacuated of its use-value; its physical existence, Marx says, then becomes "phantom-like."

It's hard to imagine that Marx, the great devourer of Shakespeare, Goethe, and Balzac, hadn't at some point read Nikolai Gogol's phantom-like tale *The Overcoat*. Gogol was already famous in Marx's day. And *The Overcoat*'s hero—or antihero—Akaky Akakievich, has his overcoat ripped off by thugs one dark night, much as Marx's *Communist Manifesto* (written six years after Gogol's tale) said market expansion (with its daylight thuggery) would tear away all veils and protective clothing of the working classes, overcoats included.

Gogol's Akaky is a lowly titular clerk, poor and passive yet silently stoic. His problem is that his overcoat is so threadbare that in places its cloth is transparent. It's nigh useless against the vicious onslaught of St. Petersburg's wind, whipping up off the Neva. Akaky fears his coat is done for. So he takes it to Petrovich, the drunken tailor "living somewhere on the third floor up some backstairs." Petrovich takes a long look at Akaky's rags and shakes his head. "No," he says, "I can't mend that. It can't be done, sir. It's too far gone." He can make a new one—for 150 rubles. Akaky's head begins to swim. How on earth will he find such a sum?

Somehow, tapping modest savings, scrimping here and there, together with an unexpected little work bonus, Akaky cobbles together the money for the new coat. And Petrovich couldn't have delivered it at a more opportune moment. The severe frost had just arrived and was set to get worse. But Akaky is warm now, and triumphant; the day of its first wearing is like a great festive holiday, Gogol says. Akaky walks taller down the street. His work colleagues, instead of pillorying him (as usual), now admire him, decked out in his majestic new garb. They organize a party in his honor.

But Akaky isn't used to these occasions and creeps away early. It's already well past his bedtime, and he's a bit tipsy after a glass of champagne. Everywhere is closed, shuttered up, and there's not a soul about the dismal streets. Suddenly, as Akaky enters a square, a pair of burly shapes dodge out of the shadows, grab Akaky's collar, punch him in the face, pull off his coat, and knee him in the groin. The overcoat has gone. Akaky calls for help—to no avail. The night watchman had seen nothing, hadn't been watching the night. Akaky runs home, "in a shocking state," says Gogol.

The next day, he goes to the police. But they're not bothered. Complain to a superior, they say, to an *important person*. (Gogol uses italics to denote *important people* in the bureaucracy.) And yet, *important persons* aren't terribly interested in hearing a poor man's grumblings about a stolen overcoat. "If I may be so bold as to trouble you, Your Excellency . . .," stammers Akaky. "Do you realize who you're talking to?" the *important person* admonishes. "Do you know who's standing before you? Do you understand? . . ." "Where did you pick up such ideas?" says the *important person*. "What is this rebelliousness spreading among the young against their chiefs and higher-ups?"

"The *important person* seemed not to notice," Gogol says, almost parenthetically, "that Akaky was already pushing fifty. And so, even if he might be called a young man, it was only relatively." Belittled by this *important person*, frozen in a raging Petersburg blizzard, on his way home Akaky catches a fever. The malady progresses violently. Akaky breathes his last a day later. "So disappeared forever," Gogol says, "a human being whom no one ever thought of protecting, who was dear to no one, in whom no one was in the least interested."

But as so often with Gogol, the end is never really the

end. Comedy lurks somewhere around the corner of trag-
edy. Akaky disappeared, until, until . . . he comes back to
life, haunting the city, this time as a phantom intent on
revenge, spending nights ripping off the overcoats of others, with no regard for rank or title, even tracking down
the *important person* himself: "Suddenly the *important
person* himself felt a violent tug at his collar . . . 'Ah, at last
I've found you!' says the phantom. 'Now I've, er, hmm,
collared you! It's your overcoat I'm after! You didn't care
a toss about mine and you couldn't resist giving me a
good ticking-off into the bargain! Now hand over your
overcoat!'" The *important person* is terrified out of his
wits. It may have been what Marx meant when he said,
in the *Communist Manifesto*, that losing your overcoat
forces you to face, "with sober senses," your "real conditions of life."

I can't help but think that Marx would have loved this
imagery of the underdog haunting the overdog. He loved
the idea of specters haunting Europe and the world,
haunting the bourgeois order, the specter of a new social
contract, a solidarity that brings justice and peace. A
phantom-thought still. But let it haunt; let it disseminate
our culture as a ghostly presence, ready to tear the coats
off the backs of *important persons*.

4.

Maybe it's not hard to visualize a ragged and moth-eaten
Marx traipsing from his dingy and cramped Dean Street
flat to his British Museum hideout. He'd be shuffling
along, incognito, through Soho's crowded backstreets,

headed for the Reading Room to plot capitalism's down-
fall, forever on the lookout for creditors and police spies.
Revolutionary hopes sustained him through his acute
penury; Marx's political calling was more important to
him than anything else, he'd said, more important than
even his health, his happiness, and his family. He'd
pass up Dean Street, across Soho Square, through narrow Sutton Row onto Charing Cross Road, up to New
Oxford Street and then Coptic Street, northward toward
Great Russell Street and, finally, climb the steps of the
museum's majestic entrance. At a good lick, it would take
fifteen minutes.

Soho in those days—between 1850 and 1856–was
densely populated, seedy and sordid, full of poverty and
slummy housing and not the trendy gentrified neighborhood it is today. (Underneath Marx's old place nowadays
is an upscale restaurant, Quo Vadis, where private diners
can hire "The Marx Room"—"an elegant, airy and ver-
satile space, perfect for lunches and dinners, weddings
and drinks parties." Fixed menus begin at £55.) In the
1850s, Soho was inhabited by hard-up bohemian types
(like Marx), writers and artists, as well as poor immigrants
from Italy and Greece (hence Greek Street), and French
Huguenots. There were market tradesmen (along Berwick
Street) and silversmiths and tailors and other artisans with
workshops. And, of course, the ubiquitous pubs.

In 1854, a cholera epidemic broke out there, killing
over 600 people. It would be one of the last to plague London. The well-known physician John Snow was on the
job, studying this outbreak. He formulated the hypoth-
esis that, in fact, the disease resulted from something in

the water supply, not airborne miasma. Soho's drinking water was contaminated by a sewer, Snow thought, and by an antiquated pump on Broad Street. Cholera wasn't picky about social class. Thus Snow's discovery prompted developments in public health and improvements in sanitation infrastructure.

Any reader of Dickens, meanwhile, would also know that in those days the other plague striking central London was *fog*. *Bleak House*, very much rooted in Marx's Dean Street era, famously opens with a set piece on the fog engulfing London, especially the poor London of "Tom-all-Alone's." Everywhere, fog reigns. Fog up the river, Dickens says, fog down the river. Fog in the eyes and throats of London's denizens: "a nether sky of fog, with fog all round them, as if they were up in a balloon and hanging in the misty clouds." On a raw afternoon, fog is rawest, and "the dense fog densest." The fog allowed people to see the city as a whole, as an egalitarian mass; but in seeing everything in shimmering white, you saw nothing. Here was a foggy world shrouded in mysterious impenetrability, an enigma for all to see yet to little comprehend. Such was the giant London of Marx and Dickens's day. To resolve the foggy murder mystery of *Bleak House*, Dickens's sleuth, Inspector Bucket, had to find his forensic way through the opaqueness.

Inspector Bucket was one of Dickens's more likable characters, an honorable man, dedicated and practical. He went about his craft with dignity and honesty, was "affable in his manners" and "innocent in this conversation—but, through the placid stream of his life, there glides an undercurrent of forefinger." Says Dickens,

"Time and place cannot bind Mr. Bucket. Like man in the abstract, he is here today and gone tomorrow—but, very unlike man indeed, he is here again the next day." And like the natural scientists of his day, such as Darwin, Bucket was on the lookout for clues, for forces and processes that aren't visible to the naked eye, but which nevertheless structure and disrupt events, and which have their own seemingly inscrutable logic.

Inspector Bucket wouldn't have been lost on Marx. Marx's own cold case, after all, was similar, and sometimes murder was involved—even if the perpetrators often weren't actually breaking the law, because they made it. Marx wanted to understand those invisible laws and enforce new ones. The fog wouldn't be lost on Marx, either, and it could easily be a metaphor for capitalist society's opaqueness, for its ability to dissimulate and occlude. It's a mist-enveloped plot involving bad guys and good guys, villains and witnesses, victims and bystanders, judge and jury. Yet it's a thoroughly modern crime, Marx said, in which social processes decouple from human agents, making it a systematic mystery where there aren't always sole perpetrators.

Inspector Marx felt inclined to spell out the difficulty of resolving such capitalist crimes: "To prevent possible misunderstandings, let me say this," he declared in his preface to the first edition of *Capital*:

> Individuals are dealt with here only in so far as they are the personifications of economic categories, the bearers of particular class-relations and interests. My standpoint from which the development of the economic

formation of society is viewed as a process of natural history, can less than any other make the individual responsible for relations whose creature he remains, socially speaking, however much he may subjectively raise himself above them.

Marx isn't interested in pointing his forefinger at individual miscreants; it is more widespread and organized criminal activity he wants to indict. He's interested in bringing down the whole capitalist mafia.

After penetrating the white foggy wall of London town, once in the British Museum Marx set himself the task of penetrating the "mystical veil" of bourgeois society, breaking through its "misty realm." Sat at his favorite pew—G7—Marx dedicated himself to a complex analysis of economic forms in which "neither microscopes nor chemical reagents are of assistance." Instead, he said, "the power of abstraction must replace both." It was thought and practice that had to plunge into the fog, and that had to come out the other side with the truth, with perceptibility.

But Marx couldn't sit long studying and writing before his carbuncles acted up. So he had to stand up periodically, move around, stretch his legs, take the pressure off his backside. He suffered from hemorrhoids, too, and from rheumatism. And in winter, he'd have to cut his day's work short, to around 3:30 p.m., because Sydney Smirke's great Reading Room had no artificial light. By day, natural light flooded in. In the fog, it might have been just as radiant as bright sunlight. Yet by afternoon, the light receded, eventually getting lost.

One of Marx's brightest concepts, perhaps his most profound dialectical construct in *Capital*, is the "fetishism of commodities." Appearing at the end of the first chapter, it tells us plenty about the "commodity-form" under capitalism; yet it also has tremendous purchase on life and knowledge in general. It emphasizes something very important about the foggy world of appearances and how people forget what lies within, what is behind the immediately apparent. We can read the fetishism of commodities as a parable in which Marx tries to bring to life (and light) the "secret" of the ostensibly trivial commodity, the genie that exists within the magic bottle.

On one level, at the level of sensuous appearance—of touch, smell, sight, taste—there's nothing mysterious about the commodity. It is as it is, a thing satisfying a need, a use-value. A strawberry is a fruit and a fruit it remains despite being embalmed in plastic on a supermarket shelf. Wood, too, continues to be wood long after it has been converted into a saleable table. On another level, though, once these useful items step forth as commodities, they "transcend sensuousness." Then, Marx says, they "stand on their head, and evolve out of their wooden brains grotesque ideas, far more wonderful than if they were to begin dancing of their own free will."

These grotesque ideas make commodities "mystical" and "enigmatic," Marx says. A commodity is created (or picked) by the actual labor of living people, who are brought together in "concrete" labor activities, employed by someone and paid a wage by someone, a capitalist. This labor is privately owned and controlled, making social items for sale and for profit. The concrete "thing-appearance" of a commodity is real enough: shoes, shirts, books, iPhones, computers, automobiles— all have very real "thing existence" in our world; we wear them, read them, touch them, tap them, and drive them. They bear quantitative price tags that adjudicate their qualitative identity. In the sensuous, perceptible realm of everyday experience, we think and deal with these objects in terms of things—exchanging one thing (money) for another thing (the commodity). This activity is very straightforward, and we seldom ponder it at any length.

But this is merely one part of the story. There's another tale to tell, says Marx, so listen up, because a commodity's physicality, its palpable thingness, bears little or no connection to the social relations that made and distribute it. We learn nothing from the commodity about productive relations between workers and owners, between minimum wage toilers and rich bosses, between factory hands and corporate CEOs, between Nike sole-makers in Vietnam and stockbrokers on Wall Street, between fourteen-year-old Foxconn girls making iPhones in China and the gleaming, billion-dollar Apple stores across the world. Intersubjective human relations, relations emerging through a particular social organization and mode of production, get perceived by people as objective.

A commodity's thing-like character disguises its social content, occludes the processes that put it in our hands. Form belies content. The masking effect, the blurring of essence by "mystical" appearance, Marx dubs *fetishism*. "It is precisely this finished form of the world of commodities," he says, "which conceals the social character of private labour and the social relations between individual workers, by making those relations appear as relations between material objects, instead of revealing them plainly." "It is nothing," Marx says, "but the definite social relation, between men themselves which assumes here, for them, the fantastic form of a relation between things."

The working class Marx described in *Capital* is still our working class; his commodity fetishism remains our commodity fetishism. Perhaps even more so. Often it involves a working class far removed from our own work lives. The Taiwanese company Foxconn has 1.3 million laborers on its payroll and employs 450,000 at its "Foxconn City" plant in Shenzhen, China, where young women put in exhausting 12-hour shifts piecing together iPhones. Most employees last only a year before burning out; worker suicides are common; survivors tell of long, grueling working days, compounded by callous managers who humiliate workers for slip-ups. Three hundred and fifty iPhones a minute are churned out. The product itself is sleek, clean, and sexy, bearing no trace of the grubby conditions that went into its production. And the trillion-dollar Apple Inc. washes its hands of its subcontractor far, far away.

Everything is forgotten, concealed behind the high-tech glitz, within the brand and fetishized in the store. Meanwhile, at the warehouses of Amazon's $800 billion empire (headed by Jeff Bezos, the world's richest man), workers clock brutal 60-hour workweeks; ambulances are frequent sights, carting out maimed workers who scurry at breakneck speeds up and down windowless warehouse aisles. They're an unseen thousand-fold army of toilers, ensuring millions of parcels of books and other paraphernalia are distributed and delivered every day, for which they're lucky to earn a minimum wage.

Marx believed conceptual analysis could demystify fetishistic visions of human experience. Like Inspector Bucket, he follows up on clues, leaves nothing unturned. But while Marx's strategy might be effective at exposing the skeletons in capitalism's closet, his urging to lay bare the real truth of our society isn't likely to go down well with the bosses. The ruling class, Marx says, is content to deceive, is "happy in its self-alienation." It has a powerful interest in maintaining the fog, in concealing what it does behind the scenes. It will do everything to propagate its myths, everything to ensure nothing tangles its purse strings. Thus the millions upon millions it spends bombarding the world with glossy ads and sophisticated campaigns to promote its goods, never letting up. All this enshrines products with the thickest, most impermeable aura that encourages us to simply go with the foggy fetishistic flow.

5.

Ever since the 1840s, Marx had interested himself in money. His vision of money was always counterintuitive, not just because he wrote about it without having any, but also because his theory of money was at odds with the classical political economists of his day—and, indeed, with the classical economists of our day. His was never a "quantitative theory of money." For Marx, it wasn't so much that money permits the circulation of commodities as the circulation of commodities expresses itself through the circulation of money, ensuring that commodities burst through all barriers of time and space, launching themselves into an orbit that is somehow, and necessarily, limitless.

Marx had his favorite refrains about money, like those he'd known as a young man in *The Economic and Philosophical Manuscripts* (1844): "Thou visible god. / That solder'st close impossibilities / And mak'st him kiss! / That speak'st with every tongue, / To every purpose! O thou touch of hearts!"

This is *Timon of Athens*, which Marx would footnote twenty years later in *Capital*. And the "visible god" in question is, of course, nothing other than money. "Shakespeare paints a brilliant picture of money," Marx insists, vividly shows the alchemy of money, how nothing is immune from money, not even "the bones of the saints can withstand it."

> Gold? Yellow, glittering, precious gold . . .
> Thus much of this will make black, white; foul, fair
> Wrong, right; base, noble; old, young; coward, valiant
> . . . What this, you gods? Why this
> Will lug your priests and servants from your sides,
> Pluck stout men's pillows from below their heads;
> This yellow slave
> Will knit and break religions; bless the accursed;
> Make the hoar leprosy adored; place thieves,
> And give them title, knee and approbation,
> With senators on the bench: this is it,

That makes the wappen'd widow wed again:
. . . Come damned earth,
Thou common whore of mankind.

Around money matters, penniless Marx also liked to recite Goethe's *Faust*, as well as Aristotle, the ancient Greek. Aristotle, says Marx, contrasted economics with "chrematistics." The former was the "art of acquisition," of obtaining articles necessary for existence, useful things for the household. They'd likely involve money to acquire them. But money here was a mere token of exchange, a facilitator that extended barter. As money became more widespread, trade followed. Money became instrumental, a means toward enlarging ends. With money you could get stuff. After a while, money unleashed those immanent contradictions that Shakespeare harked about, growing into another way of acquiring things; simple barter and a nascent money economy morphed into a more complex moneymaking economy, called chrematistics. No longer a means toward an end, money now became the end, the thing desired—the acquisition of riches for the sake of acquiring riches.

Aristotle was on to a new breed of moneybags: a *capitalist*, a person who wants to extract money from money. Aristotle never used the term capitalist; the label hadn't been invented then. In Aristotle's slave society, there were no capitalists. Not yet. They were lurking around the historic corner, taking another several thousand years to really burst through. Capitalism emerged out of a kind of chrematistics, even if the capitalist has a deeper money mania, a more modern chrematistical sickness:

the unceasing compulsion to generate profit, to acquire more and more money, to accumulate more and more capital. Before long, there's a new species of money grabber in our midst: "the rational miser," Marx calls them. Still, money circulating as mere money, and money circulating as capital, is, Marx says, "palpably different."

Indeed, Marx called his book *Capital* for good reason. Capital is more than money, even though capital secretes money, realizes itself in money. Capital is *money in process*, money that "enters into circulation, emerges from it with an increase in size, and starts the same cycle again and again. 'M-M, money which begets more money,' such is the description of capital given by its first interpreters, the Mercantilists." Buying in order to sell dear—the mantra of the merchant. Alongside the merchant, meanwhile, comes the finance capitalist, the moneylender, the loan shark, the personification of "interest-bearing capital," who fixes the terms of any money transaction at the going rate of interest—or at their own going rate of interest. Marx thinks a merchant's and financier's wealth are "derivative forms of capital," antediluvian in the development of capitalism, not the primary type of capital for modern times.

For one thing, they operate exclusively in the sphere of circulation, and Marx is adamant that "capital cannot arise from circulation." On the other hand, "It is impossible for it to arise apart from circulation." Marx likes his riddles, liking even more to resolve them: "Capital must have its origin in circulation and not in circulation." The other problem here is that the capitalist system cannot expand through merchant and finance capital alone.

Neither merchant nor finance capital create new value. Their functioning is redistributive rather than generative, not like industrialists. These forms of capital, Marx insists, involve a certain legalized *cheating*—cheating the consumer at the supermarket, cheating the borrower on the money market.

To generate capital, something at once more subtle and brutal is required. "In order to extract value out of the consumption of a commodity," Marx says,

> our friend the money-owner must be lucky enough to find within the sphere of circulation, on the market, a commodity whose use-value possesses the peculiar property of being a source of value, whose actual consumption is therefore itself an objectification of labour, hence a creation of value. The possessor of money does find such a special commodity on the market: the capacity for labour, in other words labour-power.

"The process of consumption of labour-power is," Marx says,

> at the same time the production process of commodities and of surplus-value. The consumption of labour-power is completed, as in the case of every other commodity, outside the market, or the sphere of circulation. Let us therefore, in the company with the owner of money and the owner of labour-power, leave this noisy sphere, where everything takes place on the surface and in full view of everyone, and follow them into the hidden abode of production, on whose threshold there hangs

the notice "No admittance except on business." Here we shall see, not only how capital produces, but how capital is itself produced. The secret of profit-making must at last be laid bare.

Accessing this "hidden abode," crossing its threshold to spy on capitalist production, on industrial capital's daily workings, requires negotiating more fog, groping through opaqueness. On the inside, things are gloomier, darker, and suffocatingly hot. The scene of capitalist manufacturing is mysterious and mystifying, ideologically obfuscating, purposely designed to throw any faint-hearted sleuth off the trail. Part of the fog derives from the bourgeoisie's own claims, the kind of immunity it pleads, tries to create for itself. It maneuvers for its own legitimation, hides behind a contractual basis that Marx calls a "legal fiction."

This legal fiction haughtily expresses the "innate rights" of man, of Freedom, Equality, and Property. "Freedom," says Marx, "because both buyer and seller of a commodity, let us say of labour-power, are determined only by their own free will. They contract as free persons, who are equal before the law." Equality, "because each enters into relation with one another, as with a simple owner of commodities, and they exchange equivalent for equivalent." Property, "because each disposes only of what is his own," and "because each looks only to his own advantage."

Marx caps off this conceptual shift from circulation to production with a passage that exhibits the wit peppering *Capital*, making its seriousness funny:

When we leave this sphere of simple circulation or the exchange of commodities, which provides the "free-trader *vulgaris*" with his views, his concepts and the standard by which he judges the society of capital and wage-labour, a certain change takes place, or so it appears, in the physiognomy of our *dramatis personae*. He who was previously the money-owner now strides out in front as a capitalist; the possessor of labour-power follows as a worker. One smirks self-importantly and is intent on business; the other is timid and holds back, like someone who has brought his own hide to market and now has nothing else to expect but—a tanning.

6.

We're not sure if Marx ever went into a capitalist factory, whether he ever entered or saw the hidden abode with his own eyes. Chances are, on his visits to see Engels in Manchester, he did. Perhaps Engels showed his friend around then, showed him the oily cogs and worker sweat of his father's textile manufacturing business, Ermen & Engels, in Salford. Engels had spent twenty-odd years running the plant. By day, as a capitalist, he had applied himself to Dad's factory, using some of the proceeds to subsidize Marx. By night, the communist Engels dedicated himself to overthrowing everything Dad's firm stood for. (Like everybody else living under capitalism, Engels had to deal with his own personal contradictions; and in dealing with them, he became a double-agent.)

Another source for Marx's critical image of capitalism was *testimony*. He made his case for prosecuting capitalist production by summoning the evidence of people who were closer to the crime scene. He would assemble eyewitness accounts, examine written reports, interrogate old material, and introduce new documents. He would follow up on leads, check quotes against others, cross-examine and recross-examine. Then he would piece each bit of the puzzle together, before drawing his own conclusions. Afterward, he'd make policy recommendations and revolutionary prognostications. And he did it all without ever having to leave his speck in the museum, at G7.

One of the amazing things about *Capital* is the sheer number of voices we hear talking. Marx wanted to give everybody their say, and usually he let them speak in their own tongues, frequently forked, oftentimes at length. Some people, like the economists, are sectarian and use a language intelligible only to themselves. Other voices—like the mill, mine, and factory owners—grate, and come across as callous and inhuman. Marx lets the tape run, and the more they talk, the more they dig their own graves. Still more voices belong to politicians and civil servants. They're either indifferent about committing themselves or else apologists for a system that is clearly feathering their nests. Here and there we also snatch the broken words of workers themselves, who, rather than moan indignantly, appear resigned to their lot.

Marx never deals with his characters unfairly, never quotes them speaking words they never said. He makes value judgments, for sure, intervenes in the flow of their narratives, yet nothing in Marx's larger account seems non sequitur; nothing is fabricated. He handles his subject matter as skillfully and as adroitly as the great novelists of his generation. Only this isn't fiction. His greatest resources were the "Reports of the Inspectors of Factories," commissioned by Parliament, which "provide regular and official statistics of the voracious appetite of the capitalists for surplus labour." Generated under the Home Secretary's directive, appearing twice yearly since 1835, Marx seemed to have waded through every one of them, past and present, citing vast chunks in *Capital*.

The reports were a goldmine of information, one of the few advantages of his living in England, perhaps the only advantage; the country was not only "the classic representation of capitalist production," he says, but also "the only nation to possess a continuous set of official statistics relating to the matters we are considering." To boot, the reports were openly accessible, readily available to anyone, even to the scruffy émigré Marx. (One wonders who else in his day ever studied them so attentively?) Above all else, the Inspectors' Reports shape the English Factory Acts, which, says Marx, "curb capital's drive towards a limitless draining away of labour-power by forcibly limiting the working day on the authority of the state."

Marx has no illusions about the role of the capitalist state as the executive committee "managing the common affairs of the whole bourgeoisie." But he's a revolutionary who recognizes that without the Factory Acts, and without the factory inspectors, things would be a whole lot worse for the working class. Smarter bourgeois know, too, that efforts to temper their cutthroat drive to extend the working day beyond lengths humanly possible would prevent them killing the goose that laid the golden eggs. Limiting the working day ensured that a less exhausted workforce became a more productive workforce. And if that weren't enough, some factory inspectors warned that if the government didn't properly enforce the Ten Hours' Act (1847), "class antagonisms would reach unheard of degrees of tension."

Marx portrays the manufacturers like the cast of a gothic horror story, with a "werewolf-like hunger for surplus labour," and "vampire-like, living only by sucking living labour, and living more, the more labour it sucks." The inspectors get a walk-on part as Jekyll and Hyde characters, fulfilling an ambivalent role within the state, acting as both advocate and critic. Not a few inspectors had their blood sucked out of them long ago. They turned a blind eye to their masters' infringements, to the nibbling and quibbling at worker mealtimes, pilfering minutes that should be lunch breaks and recreation times. Five minutes a day's increased work, multiplied by x number of weeks, equals several days' extra labor per year. Moments are the elements of profit.

Not all inspectors, though, were dishonest. Several were even upright, trustworthy souls, liberals who steadfastly sought to uphold the law. Among the latter was Leonard Horner, whose testimonies fill the pages of one of the pinnacle chapters of *Capital*, perhaps the pinnacle chapter, the tenth, on "The Working Day." Horner is one of the unsung heroes of his era (1785–1864), although Marx does his utmost to sing his praises. Marx could be damning of people, viciously critical, never suffering fools gladly; yet at the same time he wasn't afraid to give credit when and where it was due. And, for Marx, Horner's "services to the English working class will never be forgotten. He carried out a life-long contest, not only with the embittered manufacturers, but also with the Cabinet."

We don't know a huge amount about Horner.[5] He never lived long enough to receive Marx's compliments. Maybe, like Darwin, he'd have taken them grudgingly, been flattered yet guarded, maintaining his distance from a notorious foreign agitator. Interestingly, as a member of the Geological Society, Horner was on friendly terms with Darwin; the author of *On the Origin of Species* became a sometime visitor to the Horner household. Leonard himself was born in Edinburgh in 1785. His father was a prosperous linen merchant and Leonard entered the family business for a while. Later he worked as an underwriter in London for Lloyds insurance and then had a four-year stint (1827–31) as Warden of the newly formed University of London. The Horners were Whigish and Protestant but progressive in their belief in science and Enlightenment ideals. Thrift, hard work, and moderate asceticism were family virtues; Leonard stuck fast to this value system throughout his life.

Like Marx, he was intellectually precocious. He attended Edinburgh University as a fourteen-year-old, studying moral philosophy, math, chemistry, and geology. He read lots of classical literature, too, and read about the political and social issues of his day. A talented linguist, Leonard taught himself French, German, and Italian. He soon became a man of "formidable erudition." But Horner will be remembered, if he's ever remembered, as the longest serving and most honorable of all the early factory inspectors—a "tireless censor of the manufacturers," Marx said—on duty between 1833 and 1859 in Lancashire, the epicenter of the textile industry. By then, he was living off a private income, though probably a modest one, since his father's business had declined. Horner's employment had never been a big payer, either. Yet money doesn't appear to have been any sort of interest or motivation; Horner was driven, rather, by a sense of public duty.

He was often seen as "ruthless" by his manufacturing antagonists, and much maligned by them.[6] Incorruptible, Horner was never afraid to speak his mind in the many reports he compiled. Without his input, it would have been difficult to imagine the Ten Hours' Act ever becoming law; nor the limiting of child labor. Before Horner, nine-year-olds regularly put in fourteen-hour days. It was always an uphill struggle, he said, full of conservative obstacles and political foot-dragging. And once the legislation was enacted, somebody had to regulate it, had to keep tabs on those laws being respected. Horner was an ex-businessman himself, so in no way hostile to capitalism, nor to the desire of the mill lords wanting to make a buck. But he was morally committed to the belief that profitability could arise from good working conditions and from educating the masses.

He had his run-ins not only with the manufacturers, but also with some of the best-known political economists of his day, who balked at the idea of government intervention, especially efforts to curtail the working day. Horner's economic philosophy probably had more in common with J. S. Mill's utilitarianism than with Marx's socialism. Horner believed the aristocratic system of monopoly and privilege had to be fended off. Strong government was necessary, he said, to protect the "free market" from the unscrupulous greed that can distort it. His was a laissez-faire economics, worlds removed from Milton Friedman's and from the avaricious neoliberal deceit we know today, which has bought off most governments and created not-so-free markets everywhere. Like Mill, Horner believed markets could only ever be "free" if wide-ranging government regulation took place, assuring social as well as individual liberty.

Horner's most famous run-in regarding regulation was also one of Marx's most famous run-ins, with the Oxford political economist Nassau W. Senior. Horner's views on factory legislation were most forcefully articulated in his "open letter" to Senior, published in 1837, and endorsed by Marx. The theme was the so-called last hour of the working day. Both Horner and Marx had questioned the validity of Senior's thesis, even questioned the integrity of a "scholar," like Senior, who acted as a mouthpiece for the cotton trade. Here Horner had to remind a renowned economist, a teacher with an Ivy League Chair, that children weren't "free agents" on the labor market and needed the state to protect them from brutal factory employment. No matter where children worked, Horner told Senior, "their having a fair chance of growing up in full health and strength or with the opportunity of receiving a suitable education," was a moral right.

Senior, for Marx's part, embodied everything loathsome about English political economy, with its class bias masquerading as rigorous scholarship. This was pure ideology, Marx said, channeled through the authority of a rich, internationally renowned bourgeois institution. Thus it implicitly bore the stamp of "economic science." Marx, conversely, was an outsider, a trained philosopher yet autodidact in economic affairs. Unaffiliated and frequently destitute, sitting alone in the British Museum, he had no institutional status, no professional badge of credibility to invoke. But as an "amateur," he took to task Senior's infamous "last hour."

Marx states explicitly what Horner had only politely implied: that Oxford credentials are mobilized to legitimize flimsy scholarship; that with Senior we were witnessing the time-honored ties between the academy and industry, how each scratched the other's back. Senior had been summoned to Manchester, the seat of international textile trade, to battle for the manufacturers as their chosen "prize-fighter"; Senior's economic science was just the ammunition needed to silence struggles to reduce the factory working day. But Senior hadn't reckoned on Horner.[7]

Senior went to great technical lengths, invoking much numerical data, to argue that if the working day were reduced from twelve to ten hours all the manufacturers' profit would be destroyed. It would equally destroy the manufacturers' ability to pay their workforce, because along with profits, money for wages would go too. Everybody would lose out. In the eleventh hour, Senior said, the worker reproduced their wages and in the twelfth— the "last hour"—the manufacturers' profit. To cut the working day to ten hours would thus eliminate both. As Marx says, "and the Professor calls this 'analysis'!"

These are "extraordinary notions," Marx writes, and spends pages carefully denouncing prejudice dressed up as economic science. Senior grovels before the manufacturers, Marx says: "The heart of a man is a wonderful thing, especially when it is carried in his wallet." At one point, the Oxford professor even tries to give scientific credence to exploiting child labor. There's a "warm and moral atmosphere in the factory," Senior says, which keeps children out of mischief and vice, beyond the grip of their idle parents. Marx, like Horner, questioned the accuracy of Senior's figures. And, he says, "apart from errors in its content, Senior's presentation is confused."

Profit results from "surplus labour time," of course; the time workers spend beyond the "necessary labour time" of earning their wages and recuperating manufacturers' overheads. The longer the working day and the lower the wages, the greater the surplus labor amassed. Surplus labor time is the source of "surplus-value," and surplus-value is, in turn, the real source of profit—all of which has absolutely nothing to do with any "last hour" of work. Thus "this faithful 'last hour,' about which you have invented more stories than the millenarians about the Day of Judgment, is," Marx concludes, "all bosh."

7.

Overwork remains a major problem for working people. So long as capitalism sucks blood from living labor, it persists as a death warrant for producing surplus-value. In his "Working Day" chapter, Marx recounts the demise of Mary Anne Walkley, a twenty-year-old garment worker who, in June 1863, toiled on average sixteen and a half hours a day without a break, often as much as thirty hours straight. The "flow of her failing 'labour-power,'" Marx says, "is maintained by occasional supplies of sherry, port and coffee." Mary Anne was busy "conjuring up magnificent dresses for the noble ladies invited to the ball in honour of the newly imported Princess of Wales." After twenty-six and a half hours of straight toil, done in a small, stifling sweatshop, with thirty other girls, Mary Anne fell ill on a Friday and was dead by Sunday, "without, to the astonishment of Madame Elise, having finished off the bit of finery she was working on." "Death from simple overwork," was the verdict in the following day's newspaper.

On March 8, 1997—International Women's Day—Carmelita Alonzo, a thirty-five-year-old mother of five, suffered a similarly gruesome fate at a Philippines factory, stitching garments for VT (Vitorio Tan) Fashion Image, Inc., a subcontractor of the clothing chain Gap. She died at the Andres Bonifacio Memorial Hospital in Cavite, Philippines, after eleven days in intensive care. According to her co-workers at VT Fashion, "Carmelita was killed by her 14-hour workday every day plus overtime of eight hours every Sunday."

In July 2013, Miwa Sado, a thirty-one-year-old journalist, working for Japan's public broadcasting corporation, logged 159 hours of overtime and took only two days a month off on the run-up to her death from heart failure. In April 2014, likewise in Japan, Joey Tocnang, a twenty-seven-year-old trainee at a metal casting company, died in the firm's dormitory, after a similarly punishing work schedule finally took its toll. Japanese authorities said his "death was directly related to the long hours of overtime he was forced to perform." He'd been working between 78.5 and 122.5 hours of overtime every month, cutting steel and preparing casts of molten metal, sending home his meager salary to his wife and five-year-old daughter in the Philippines.[8] In April 2015, Matsuri Takahashi, a twenty-four-year-old employee at the Japanese advertising conglomerate Dentsu, did herself in before work got to her first, committing suicide after regularly working more than a hundred hours a month overtime. She posted a message on social media a few weeks before she died, saying, "I want to die . . . I'm physically and mentally shattered."[9]

The Japanese have a name for this—*karōshi*, death from overwork. Japanese companies expect employees to put in long hours in a fiercely competitive workplace culture. Workers are cajoled into clocking up mammoth hours, proving their dedication to the job as well as their loyalty to the company. The government says one in five workers in Japan are now at risk from overwork—from strokes and heart attacks to mental illnesses and suicides. The Japanese health ministry reported ninety-three cases of suicides or attempted suicides in early 2016 directly linked to work pressure. And the national police agency said overwork was likely responsible for 2,159 suicides in 2015.

Overwork is rife in Britain as well. In 2016, 40 percent of working Brits didn't take their full holiday entitlement; one in six employees had a full working week of unused holidays to spare. Seven out of ten British workers drag themselves out of their sickbed to go to work (the majority presumably because they're not paid otherwise). The number of people working over forty-eight hours per week has doubled in Britain since 1998, up from 10 percent to 26 percent. Overwork problems hit the working privileged, who feel they must rack up the hours to advance their careers, as well as the working desperate, who have little choice but to toil to make ends meet, often at more than one job. Studies illustrate how output significantly trails off after a fifty-hour workweek, and nose dives after fifty-five hours. (They also show that people who regularly work more than forty-nine hours a week are at a significantly higher risk of strokes.)

In the United States, there's no such thing as Senior's "last hour" simply because there's no obligation for employers to limit the working day. The limit, one assumes, is when you drop. Leonard Horner would have had his work cut out as a labor inspector; but given there are no regulators now, nor any future openings for labor inspectors, his own hours would be drastically slashed. Americans, on the whole, work longer hours and have more stress-related work illnesses than their European counterparts, even more than Japanese workers, which is hard to imagine.[10] Reasons are due to stagnating wages and to hopelessly outdated overtime laws.

But the problem is writ large, too, in the tech industry and in finance jobs, which are always trying to motivate workers to hustle more and work harder. No matter how seductive and "happy" the workplace is, today's reality remains Marx's reality: employees are human widgets used and discarded at the behest of bosses. What counts for a firm is your VORP—"Value Over a Replacement Player." You're indispensable so long as there's nobody else around who can perform better, who's more compliant, and who's more able to work even harder and longer than you. "Companies burn you out and churn you up when somebody better, or cheaper, becomes available."[11]

At HubSpot, a high-tech start-up in Cambridge, Massachusetts, there's a slick and happy veneer "with bean-bag chairs and unlimited vacation—a corporate utopia where there's no need for work-life balance because work is life and life is work. Imagine a frat house mixed with a kindergarten mixed with Scientology, and you have an idea of what it's like."[12] But despite the cool office interior there's no job security. It's a typical digital sweatshop where young workers, packed side by side at long tables, hunch over laptops rather than sewing machines, staring into them for hours and hours, barking commands into headsets, trying to sell software, selling themselves in the process. "The free snacks are nice," one ex-employee said, "but you must tolerate having your head stuffed with silly jargon and ideology about being on a mission to change the world. Wealth is generated, but most of the loot goes to a handful of people at the top."

Tech software work pales, however, compared to tech hardware work, which is usually just that—hard—frequently done thousands of miles away from any hip Silicon Valley paradise. Over in China, at Foxconn again, in Shenzhen, there has been a spate of worker suicides, all overwork-related. One male worker hanged himself in a Foxconn toilet in 2007; in 2009, another threw himself from his apartment window, after being beaten by

Foxconn managers. In 2010, fifteen employees (eleven men, four women) killed themselves. In 2011, four; in 2012, one; in 2013, two. More recently, on January 6, 2017, Li Ming jumped to his death in Zhengzhou, where he worked for Foxconn, no longer able to endure his working life there.

Meanwhile, Foxconn's child labor practices take us back to *Capital*. The company was recently found recruiting more than a thousand schoolchildren to work nights, making Amazon's Alexa devices—the virtual voice gadgets used to control lights and domestic appliances. These kids are classified as "student interns," there to cover labor shortages and trim costs. Sixteen-year-olds toil ten hours a day, six days a week, on the production line, receiving 16.55 yuan ($2.39) an hour, compared to the 20.18 yuan per hour for regular employees. They have little choice in the matter. If students refuse to work the designated hours, including the compulsory overtime, their teachers tell them it will affect their graduation chances and scholarship opportunities. Foxconn defends its use of schoolchildren: "It provides students," they say, "who are all of a legal work age, with the opportunity to gain practical work experience and on-the-job training in a number of areas that will support their efforts to find employment following their graduation."[13]

This notion that hard work is healthy for kids harks back to the workhouses of a certain "Dr." Andrew Ure, another quack bourgeois political economist from Marx's day—and ardent cheerleader of Nassau Senior. Ure, said Marx, "argued that if children and young persons under 18 years of age, instead of being kept the full 12 hours in the warm and pure moral atmosphere of the factory, are turned out an hour sooner into the heartless and frivolous outer world, they will be deprived, owing to idleness and vice, of all hope of salvation of their souls."[14] The Foxconn of *Capital*'s era was Sanderson Bros. & Co., a steel rolling mill and forge in Sheffield. Boss E. F. Sanderson admitted "great difficulty would be caused by preventing boys of under 18 from working at night. The chief would be the increased cost from employing men instead." Besides, it would be impossible, Sanderson said, to leave such expensive machinery idle half the time, working only throughout daylight hours. The training that his company gave to an apprentice, he bragged, should be considered "part of the return for the boys' labour. . . . Boys must begin young to learn a trade," and to learn their station in life.

8.

Back in the mid-1990s, when I lived in central London, I used to walk past the British Museum nearly every day. More often than not, I'd pop in, did so for years, getting thrilled by a couple of things. The first, obviously, was entering the great Reading Room, for which I had a Reader's Card, glimpsing and even sitting in space G7. I never ordered any books, had no need to order anything; all I wanted was to sit there, in Marx's seat, and try to feel the vibe. Usually, there wasn't any vibe, only the hushed shuffling and page-turning of others close by, mixed with the odd cough and splutter. The atmosphere was bookish and musty. No PCs were in sight. It was pencil and paper stuff in those days. I tried to imagine Marx scribbling away, muttering to himself, piling up those Inspectors' Reports in front of him, working frantically on *Capital*. Doing so, I remember, was strangely comforting.

Afterward, my other great delight was visiting the "old" Reading Room, with its permanent display of "literary treasures." Glass cabinets housed original handwritten drafts of Dickens's *Nicholas Nickleby*, Lewis Carroll's *Alice in Wonderland*, William Wordsworth's poem "Composed Upon Westminster Bridge," and Charlotte Brontë's *Jane Eyre*. But the treasure that thrilled me most was one of James Joyce's notebooks of *Finnegans Wake*—from the 1930s, when Joyce was still cagey about its title; for years he'd called it simply "Work in Progress." The writing, in soft pencil, was chaotic and sprawling, and as mad as Marx's handwritten scrawl. Like the drafts of *Capital*, there was as much crossed out as left legible. Joyce used thick colored crayons (orange and green were favorites) to score out sentences, sometimes whole pages that he seemed not to want—until he informed someone that he crossed out what he wanted, but had already used elsewhere, in another more definitive version.

In those years, Marx and Joyce were my heroes; they still are. But it's perhaps only now that I realize curious similarities between each man. After all, they both had an obsession with wanting to include everything in their work, constantly adding to it, expanding and inserting material, making it seemingly impossible for them ever to finish anything. Like Marx, Joyce was a publisher's nightmare, forever making last-minute insertions into the proofs. After he'd eventually published *Ulysses*, his benefactor, Harriet Weaver, asked him what he planned on doing next. Joyce responded that he wanted "to write a history of the world."

Marx had a similar lofty ambition for *Capital*, likewise attempting to write a history of the world, incorporating everything, seeking the same organic unity and wholeness that *Finnegans Wake* sought. Capital circulated through Marx the same way as the Liffey circulated through Joyce: "a commodius vicus of recirculation." In a sense, each book is a "hyper-text," a big, intricately entangled, introverted yet expansive text, historical yet somehow universal, exuberant and imaginative, and at times colossally difficult to understand. Joyce said his principal character, H. C. Earwicker, was a "fargazer," whose "patternmind" dreamed the vastest dream, whose sigla H.C.E. meant "Here Comes Everybody."

Capital was Marx's fargazing, a condition, he thought, where all countries were headed, his image of everybody's future. He sketched the historical and geographical mission of the capitalist mode of production, with its need to create industrial cities, to move mountains, to dig canals, to connect everywhere, to nestle everywhere. Within it all, Marx believed that a physical and emotional proximity of workers would be created; a common experience among workers, even if they were hundreds or even thousands of miles apart. This common experience would be a sort of cosmopolitanism, a global solidarity, a Here Comes Everybody.

In the summer of 2019, I returned to the British Museum. A lot had changed since the mid-1990s; a big,

postmodern overhaul had taken place, leaving a spar-
kling new design and a sort of canopy spread across
Sydney Smirke's Reading Room. Everything was now
bright cream and a new skylight enclosed an open public forum—"The Great Court," Europe's largest covered
square, inaugurated in 2000—which was packed full
with tourists. Dominated by a sprawling museum store,
it felt like a glorified shopping mall. I tried to get into the
Reading Room, through a puny little corridor, following the route I used to know; but barriers where placed
across, preventing any public entrance. "No Entry" signs
were emblazoned everywhere. In fact, everybody, staff
included, seemed barred.

I asked one of the museum ushers what was happening, "Why can't you access the Reading Room anymore?" "It had been closed for ages," he said. "Is it being
refurbished?" I wondered. He didn't know. "They don't
tell us anything." I mused on who "they" might be. I
asked someone else at the "Information" booth. She was
sour, seemed suspicious of my questioning, and didn't
know anything, repeating what I'd earlier heard: "They
don't tell us anything."

I asked a third member of staff, at the "Membership"
zone, who was friendlier. In her heavy Eastern European accent, she told me the Reading Room had been
closed since 2000, since the time of the refurbishment.
"For nineteen years!" I exclaimed. "Yes," she said. She
didn't know what was happening either. I asked her who
employed the staff at the museum and she said it was a
subcontractor; only a minority of people actually work
"in-house" for the museum. Cleaners and other auxiliary

staff are mostly outsourced labor.[15] I felt the alienation in the air, alienation in the place where Marx wrote about alienation, and departed despondent, struck by the irony, and disillusioned about the times in which we live.

The entire book and manuscript collection, once stored in the Reading Room, had been relocated in 1998, up the road, to the new British Library, next to St. Pancras Station. The pressing problem, apparently, was lack of shelf space at the old British Museum. It had been a "legal deposit," meaning it received every book published in the UK, including many overseas titles. It needed an extra two kilometers of shelving every year, which the new British Library, reputedly the largest national library in the world, can now offer. All the "literary treasures" have been transferred to the British Library, too, and that got me wondering about my old *Finnegans Wake* treasure, those notebooks from years ago.

So I wandered over to the library, but in the new display section, impressively organized and expanded—to include the *Magna Carta* and rare editions of the Bible— there was no Joyce. Ted Hughes and Sylvia Plath were new additions, "younger" writers added to the modernist canon; yet it seemed Jim had been bumped off. Somebody told me at the Information desk that if he wasn't on display then he's probably in storage. Some texts, she said, needed a "rest," so Joyce was likely resting. *Finnegans Wake* needing a rest? It was about a sleeping man! No Marx's seat, no *Finnegans Wake* notebook—the times were a-changing, and it didn't seem to me they were moving in the right direction.

Somehow, the experience of Marx in the museum

began to strike me as more vital than ever. I'm not just talking here about Marx the revolutionary; I'm talking about Marx the dedicated scholar, Marx the restless yet patient analyst of reports, documents, and texts of all kinds; Marx the inquirer of truth, I mean, the Dickensian sleuth searching for answers, the solver of mysteries, the man who wants to cut through the fog. Indeed, so much of what he presents in *Capital* involves the lies and misinformation of others, the bourgeois propaganda that lurks behind the apparent seal of knowledge. Marx wanted to disperse these ideological smokescreens. He wanted to demonstrate a certain truthfulness and got pilloried by his right-wing antagonists for it.

I say we need Marx more than ever because we've had assorted demagogues in recent years persuade masses of people that they have nothing in common anymore. These demagogues have been rather frivolous with the truth; in fact, they've profited from a plurality of truths, many of which aren't truthful at all. It's especially hard now to pass rational critical judgment. Telling the truth requires courage and great skill, and often considerable energy to sift through the lies saturating us morning, noon, night, and much of the time in between. Most disturbing of all, perhaps, is people's willingness to believe these political falsehoods, even when they know they aren't true.

Marx had no illusions about the struggle around knowledge production and its dissemination. He knew that we can never prevent politicians and businesspeople from lying. They have the means and the media to do so. But Marx hoped that, maybe one day, we could create the social conditions whereby people's need to believe in the miraculous lie might somehow whither away. To call on people to give up illusions about our condition is, he thought, to make a call to give up a condition that requires illusions.

We live in foggy times. The Nassau W. Seniors, Andrew Ures, and E. F. Sandersons are still among us, those characters we hear in *Capital*, those moneybags and ideologues and mill lords accumulating capital at other people's expense. Their names are different, they look different, but what they do isn't so different: it was, always will be, simply a pretext for profit-making, for extracting surplus-value. Marx conceived this in a museum that is no longer accessible. The museum is effectively gone. The need for Marx has apparently gone. He has no seat among us anymore. But his vision of what is wrong and what might be right with our society gathers no dust.

9.

The longest chapter in *Capital* is the fifteenth, on "Machinery and Large-Scale Industry." At almost 150 pages, it's really a book in itself, a staggeringly dense and expansive discussion that could easily stand alone—not only as a brilliant exegesis of capitalist machinery, but also as a sweeping social history of technology. At its broadest reach, the chapter is a vivid demonstration of historical materialism in action, of Marx's method put through its dialectical paces. As ever with Marx, his footnotes aren't to be passed over glibly: they're worth studying, pondering over for the nuggets of insight they contain.

His intent is expressed early on, in footnote 4, where Marx suggests that what's crucial here is to write a "critical history of technology." He writes: "Darwin directed attention to the history of natural technology, i.e. to the formation of the organs of plants and animals, which serve as the instruments of production for sustaining their life." Doesn't, then, "the history of the productive organs of man in society, of organs that are the material basis of every particular organization of society, deserve equal attention?" Footnote 4 is especially rich, buried away for all but the most meticulous reader to fully absorb: "Technology reveals the active relation of man to nature," Marx tells us, "the direct process of the production of his life, and thereby it also lays bare the process of the production of the social relations of his life, and of the mental conceptions that flow from those relations."

Marx goes on, digging still deeper:

> Even a history of religion that is written in abstraction from this material basis is uncritical. It is, in reality, much easier to discover by analysis the earthly kernel of the misty creations of religion than to do the opposite, i.e. to develop from the actual, given relations of life the forms in which these have been apotheosized. The latter method is the only materialist, and therefore the only scientific one. The weaknesses of the abstract materialism of natural science, a materialism which excludes the historical process, are immediately evident from the abstract and ideological conceptions expressed by its spokesmen whenever they venture beyond the bounds of their own specialty.

Once again, Marx's desire is to cut through the ideological fog, to get at the "earthly kernel," to displace
"misty creations," and develop a grounded and critical analysis of technology. Humans make machines, he
says, develop technology from bright ideas. Always have
done, always will do. Bright ideas, however, don't just
spring from up above, from the heavens, but emerge out
of prevailing material circumstances. Yet as soon as those
bright ideas are realized materially, get embodied in new
technology, in new machinery, they react, help shape us
in dramatically ambivalent ways. We make the technology; technology remakes us. Technology changes prevailing ideas, too, which then open further possibilities
for the development of other new ideas, and other new
technological advancements.

Note here that Marx may be fascinated by technology but he's no technological determinist. Actually, little in
Marx's universe is ever *determined*. Technology *conditions*
the parameters of our lives at a given moment in time; it
doesn't determine our lot, control our fate. Technology
may be benign in itself, and commercial proponents of
technology always happily insist upon it; but because, in
human society, there's no such thing as "in itself," technology can never be benign. Its development over time
has been something of a "revealing" social process: from
the development of the steam engine to the ubiquity of the
World Wide Web, technology has revealed a certain stage
of human advancement, a certain way in which we relate to
one another, exploit one another, know one another.

Marx is well versed in the history of technology and
seems to have read everything on the topic. There are

references galore in chapter 15, hundreds of sources cited and reports consulted. He plainly thinks technology is paramount in our lives, particularly since the invention of the spinning machine and steam engine. Technology mediates our "metabolism" with nature, Marx says, mediates our productive transformation of the natural world. Since the beginning of time, we've interacted with nature, made tools to shape nature, confronted the material forces of nature and appropriated them as a force of our own nature. By acting upon external nature and changing it, we've invented a human nature, Marx says. This is why he places so much stress on the act of productive human labor. Humans make modes of production, so they're not beyond our reach to control or change. This might seem obvious, but Marx's point here is that there's nothing God-given or "natural" about capitalism. We have the capacity to fix technology, to transform the mode of production. Through the exertion of our working organs, our own bodies, our arms and legs, our heads and hands, our physical and mental powers, we've consciously created the people we are today, as well as the world we live in. This creation is always ongoing, never a done deal.

Technology is a vital force of production: from primitive tools to more complex instruments of specialized handicraft, from beaters and combers, tanners and cobblers, shearers and spinners, manufacture and combined mechanization, to fully automated factories and microchip technology—all have defined the development of different epochs of human history. Each epoch somehow strives to go beyond its own technological limits: "When a system had attained a certain degree of development," Marx says,

> it had to overthrow this ready-made foundation, which had meanwhile undergone further development to its old form, and create for itself a new basis appropriate to its own mode of production. Just as the individual machine retains a dwarf-like character as long as it is worked by the power of man alone, and just as no system of machinery could be properly developed before the steam-engine took the place of earlier motive powers . . . so too large-scale industry was crippled in its whole development as long as its characteristic instrument of production, the machine, owed its existence to personal strength and personal skill, and depended on the muscular development, the keenness of sight and the manual dexterity with which the specialized workers, in manufacture, and the handicraftsmen outside manufacture, wielded their dwarf-like implements.

Thus large-scale industry replaced isolated machines by developing them into an organized system. Often, when Marx talks about the mechanized factory system, his prose sounds Gothic, like Mary Shelley's *Frankenstein* (published the year of his birth, 1818), with its ghost in the machine. Inanimate objects take on a terrifying vitality of their own. As dead labor, they come alive to wreak havoc on animate bodies, on puny living labor: "In place of the isolated machine, a mechanical monster whose body fills whole factories, and whose demonic power, at first hidden by the slow and measured motions of its gigantic members, finally bursts forth in the fast and feverish whirl of its countless working organs."

It doesn't take Marx long before he casts his critical gaze upon capitalism's mechanical monsters. Here demonic technology becomes yet another pretext for producing surplus-value. Insofar as machinery dispenses with muscular power, shouldn't it lighten the load, actually make work easier? Sensible people would have thought so, and plenty of political economists began arguing as much, often with noble, if naïve, intention. Marx was the first, and most vociferous, to twist the logic around, to point out the "economic paradox," that "the most powerful instrument for reducing labour-time suffers a dialectical inversion and becomes the most unfailing means for turning the whole lifetime of the worker into labour-time at capital's disposal for its own valorization."

With new labor-saving technology, the "civil war" over the working day opens a new front. Henceforth, exploitation isn't just blatantly absolute: now it's necessarily relative as well. Indeed, any potential gain made by labor to restrict the working day—through the Ten Hours' Bill, collective bargaining, union drives, strike actions, etc.—are destined to be offset by ratcheting up the intensity and productivity of work, making the job faster and more efficient within a set time frame. This extra productivity Marx calls "relative surplus-value." "By an increase in the productivity of labour," he says, "we mean an alteration in the labour process of such a kind as to shorten the labour-time socially necessary for the production of a commodity, and to endow a given quantity of labour with the power of producing a greater quantity of use-value."

The sheer numbers of workers brought together, now cooperating in a factory, creates a new, intrinsically collective, power. On the one hand, it highlights the tremendous potential of modern men and women to make life fruitful. Yet, on the other hand, this radiant dream sadly becomes merely "another driving motive and determining purpose of capitalist production." The "free-gift" of collective labor undergoes ever-greater sophistication when cooperative work is divided up into discrete tasks within a division of labor. All liberating connections rip apart and metamorphose into alienating separations. What capital gains in kind, a worker loses in substance, since repetition and uniform activity "disturbs the intensity and flow of a man's vital forces, which find recreation and delight in change of activity itself."

Cooperation and the division of labor reach a higher level of efficiency with the advent of mechanical invention. The ante is upped once machines and technological knowledge burst onto the scene. Now, instruments of man only betoken man the instrument. In theory, machines lessen the burden. In reality, they become an "alien power," more frantically setting in motion labor-power, transforming people into mere appendages of mechanical devices, crippling true subjectivity, ushering in the "real subsumption" of life under the domain of capital. Even the lightening of any labor turns into "an instrument of torture, since the machine does not free the worker from work, but rather deprives the work itself of all content." Work, we might say, gets lean and stupid, at least for the bulk of workers; and an increased expenditure of labor and heightened intensity of labor-power achieves "a closer filling-up of the pores of the working day."

These contradictions, needless to say, don't arise from the machinery itself, "but out of their capitalist application. Therefore, since machinery in itself shortens the hours of labour, but when employed by capital it lengthens them; since in itself it lightens labour, but when employed by capital it heightens its intensity; since in itself it is a victory of man over the forces of nature but in the hands of capital it makes man the slave of these forces; since in itself it increases the wealth of the producers, but in the hands of capital it makes them paupers." Remember, the United States, the most technologically advanced nation, leads the world in hours worked. The workweek continues to grow longer and longer because of time-saving ingenuity. The workday pores have filled up accordingly, spurring hefty productivity hikes. This is hardly surprising, given that cellular phones, email, laptops, and various hand-held electronic devices permit lots of people to work while they're traveling to work, to work at home, on vacation, at their leisure, to their heart's content.

Instruments of labor, in the form of giant machines, quickly become competitors to workers. Such is Marx's stance. For one thing, machines become the most powerful weapons for suppressing strikes, "those periodic revolts of the working class against the autocracy of capital." The steam-engine was the first antagonist of "human power," Marx says, an antagonist that "enabled the capitalists to tread underfoot the growing demands of workers," especially those rallying to limit the working day. "It would be possible," Marx quips, "to write a whole history of the inventions made since 1830 for the sole purpose of providing capital with weapons against working class revolt."

The other thing about technology is that with it a worker's productive days are numbered; superfluity beckons. This is Marx's first mention of an idea he'd later deepen, in chapter 25, under the rubric "the general law of capitalist accumulation": the progressive production of a relative surplus population. Like paper money thrown out of currency by legal enactment, with the advent of new machine technology, Marx says, human beings themselves become unsalable, no longer directly necessary for the self-valorization of capital, losing both their use-value and exchange-value capacity. Now labor-power is dispensable and disposable, expelled from one branch of industry, attracted to another, pushed and shoved and cajoled into others, swamping lower-rung labor-markets, depressing the overall price.

Marx seems to guess what lies in store for these workers; his language even has a contemporary ring: "Every branch of industry attracts each year a new stream of men, who furnish a contingent from which to fill up vacancies, and to draw a supply for expansion." To the "great consolation" of these "pauperized workers," their sufferings, he says, mocking bourgeois apologists, "are only temporary, 'a temporary inconvenience.'" These days, most of us have heard assorted economists and politicians brag about Information

Technology single-handedly raising productivity, cutting costs for business, and allowing economies to grow, lowering unemployment and creating work for people. Marx would turn this rationale on its head, puncturing such techno-fetishism.

He would see increased accumulation residing in increased exploitation, in the diminution of living labor, in the progressive production of irregular, insecure, low-paid work. He'd likewise dispel a few myths about his own class analysis en route. "The extraordinary increase in the productivity of large-scale industry," he says, "accompanied as it is by both a more intensive and a more extensive exploitation of labour-power in all spheres of production, permits a larger and larger part of the working class to be employed unproductively." By "unproductive" he means "servant classes," "domestic slaves," "lackeys," which constantly expand in numbers. We can perhaps update these occupational groupings, interpret them today as home-care workers and cleaners, as check out clerks and restaurant workers, as janitors and security guards, as hamburger flippers and delivery men and women.

When Marx wrote *Capital*, the largest working-class faction was not in fact blue-collar factory workers, but an "unproductive" servant class. In England and Wales in the 1860s, he notes, those employed in textile factories, mines and metal industries, taken together, were "less than the number of domestic modern slaves." "What an elevating consequence of the capitalist exploitation of machinery!" he exclaims. The logic is counterintuitive yet crucial: technological expansion of the productive forces actively creates an unproductive service-sector class. As the mode of production advances, what looks like the disappearance of the "traditional" working class is, in actuality, a reconstitution of this traditional working class, a working class that is really swelling its ranks. The growth of a service class reflects a deepening of capital-labor relations, not its supersession. That we are nowadays said to be living in a high-tech, "post-industrial" society is definitive proof of Marx's class theory—not a reason to abandon it. Capitalism was always post-industrial, even back in the 1860s. From the get-go, tertiarization was immanent in its process of proletarianization.[16]

10.

"Machinery and Large-Scale Industry" is not only *Capital*'s longest chapter, it's also its most dialectical. Contradiction and conflict infuse the narrative, give it its vitality, pushing and pulling the reader along in all manner of different directions. Marx's own ambivalence reflects technology's ambivalence, and though what he's writing about is obviously rooted in his own times, it's surely not hard to relate this ambivalence to the technology that infuses our times.

Marx acknowledges that "modern industry" is both thrilling and scary, revolutionary and progressive:

> Modern industry never views or treats the existing form of a production process as the definitive one. Its technical basis is therefore revolutionary, whereas all earlier modes of production were essentially conservative.

By means of machinery, chemical processes and other methods, it is continually transforming not only the technical basis of production, but also the functions of the worker and the social combinations of the labour process. At the same time, it thereby revolutionizes the division of labour, and incessantly throws masses of capital and of workers from one branch of production to another.

And yet, that selfsame modern industry is brutal, too, inflicting immense suffering on the working class who operate it, doing away

with all repose, all fixity and all security as far as the worker's life-situation is concerned; how it constantly threatens, by taking away the instruments of labour, to snatch from his hands the means of subsistence, and, by suppressing his specialized function, to make him superfluous. We have seen, too, how this contradiction bursts forth without restraint in the ceaseless human sacrifices required from the working class, in the reckless squandering of labour-powers, and in the devastating effects of social anarchy. This is the negative side.

Marx brings together the soft and hard realities of modern life. On the one hand, the subjective human element, of what happens to the pliable worker, as living labor, when they encounter technology; on the other hand, an objective side, of what machinery itself represents under capitalism, how it functions as a physical repository of value, as dead labor, as constant capital.

On the human front, Marx makes it clear that all capitalist technology will likely enervate the body and mind of workers. "Factory work exhausts the nervous system to the utmost," he says. "At the same time, it does away with the many-sided play of muscles, and confiscates every atom of freedom, both in bodily and in intellectual activity." "The technical subordination of the worker to the uniform motion of the instruments of labour," Marx adds, "gives rise to a barrack-like discipline."

Now, it's true that the factory system Marx describes here, with its "barrack-like discipline," might be a blast from Western nations' past, a relic of their former "Fordist" mass-producing glory days, between the 1930s and 1960s; but over in China, with its burgeoning mega-Fordist factory system, Marx's analysis sounds as fresh as ever. (Even the Chinese government speaks a triumphalist rhetoric that echoes Marx's nineteenth-century English boosters.) Maybe more significant, though, is that those specific traits of the factory system have, these days, entered into the generic traits of society writ large. Thus factories might be disappearing through deindustrialization, yet their logic has seeped into everyday life. Whether inside or outside the factory, every form of labor has now been reduced to a kind of industrial labor, to dispensable labor-power, with its work drills and efficiency targets, its speedups and intensity drives, all designed to fill in those leaky workday pores.

Even high-tech work, as we've seen, resembles a sweatshop. In fact, if anything, new technology enables even more despotic surveillance and discipline. And the idea that work uses up the body and mind is apparently true for lots of twenty-first-century employees. Frequently, work becomes a torture and dread zone because it is so utterly deprived of any content, is so senseless and meaningless for those who carry it out, enervating body and spirit. It lasts too long as well, and nobody would miss it if it were ever abolished.

Every year in Europe, Repetitive Strain Injury (RSI) at work increases 20 percent. In keyboard-tapping offices and checkout-scanning supermarkets, RSI rises as much as 50 percent each year. In 2017, 4.5 million Canadians and 1.4 million Brits were affected by work-related RSI. The U.S. Bureau of Labor Statistics reckons nearly two-thirds of all occupational illnesses reported in 2017 were caused by RSI (most notably in the wrist, elbow, and shoulder), affecting 8 million American workers every year. While women represent 45 percent of the overall U.S. workforce, they account for 75 percent of RSI. (Carpal Tunnel Syndrome, a painful compression of the nerve as it passes across the front of the wrist, accounts for half of all RSI cases.) This is what happens, Marx might have said, when humans are forced "to identify themselves with the unvarying regularity of the complex automaton."

Marx pinpoints the fallacy of technology, even on its own terms. At first glance, new technology and machinery seem to raise productivity. By deploying new technology capitalists can gain an edge over competitors. Yet those effects are usually short-lived, lasting only until a competitor reciprocates. But there's mystification here, too, because machinery, says Marx, while entering into the whole of the labor process, "enters only piece by piece into the process of valorization. It never adds more value than it loses, on average, by depreciation." Like every other component of "constant capital," machinery creates no new value. Constant capital, Marx explains, is the part of capital turned into means of production, into the raw material and instruments of labor, into the machinery and auxiliary inputs that "don't undergo any quantitative alteration of value in the process of production."

Adopting new technology is a costly and risky business for any capitalist, invariably an upheaval that involves the destruction of old constant and fixed capital, the ripping out of archaic machinery, the transformation of former warehousing, casting everything past aside, into the dustbin of history, throwing in one's lot with new devices, with new instruments of labor. It's one reason why capitalists get twitchy when expensive machinery lies idle or isn't functioning to maximum capacity. They want it operational day and night, without interruption, thrashing out productivity, maybe not realizing that diminishing returns are already setting in.[17]

Marx suggests deterioration of machinery takes three forms. One arises from use, or rather from overuse, a piece of machinery that wears out just as coins wear out through being in active circulation. Another sort of deterioration is the flip side, caused by lack of use, "as a sword rusts when left in its scabbard." In addition to wear and tear or rusting up, Marx says machinery can undergo a third type of depreciation, more common under capitalism. And it's nothing physical, not initially; more a conscious boardroom decision. Marx uses an odd term to describe it: "*moral depreciation*." Here, he says, a means of production "loses exchange-value, either because machines of the same sort are being produced more cheaply than it was, or because better machines are entering into competition with it."

Almost every aspect of deindustrialization since the 1970s stems from moral depreciation. The rusted machinery, the broken windows of the redundant town plant, the rats gnawing away inside the warehouses, the weeds pushing through the loading docks, the forlorn sense of abandonment we've seen everywhere in the old manufacturing heartlands of Europe and America—rarely has any of it had anything to do with under or overuse. It's been a very capitalist morality play, the explicit devaluation of the means of production because those means of production weren't valorizing enough. Moral depreciation frequently means revaluation through relocation, since the value embodied in old constant and fixed capital can't be rebooted without being destroyed. All that is solid melts into air.[18]

Innovation becomes compulsive for any competitive capitalist, the perpetual yearning to outdo a rival, to break a rival, to monopolize a market. Science is complicit in gaining this edge, in the technological expediency of production. Marx, accordingly, casts a justly skeptical eye over the institution of science, recognizing its ability to promote life while knowing it is also a darker, Faustian force, yet another element of the competitive process. In the *Grundrisse*—raw notebooks from 1857/8, parts of which were eventually distilled into *Capital*—Marx notes how "the accumulation of knowledge and of skill, of the general productive forces of the social brain is thus absorbed into capital." In *Capital*, note 23 of chapter 15, he says, "Generally speaking, science costs the capitalist nothing, a fact that by no means prevents him from exploiting it. 'Alien' science is incorporated by capital just as 'alien' labour is." Production blossoms through the technological application of science, driving productivity onward, yet ushering in moral depreciation around some not too distant corner.

Many of Marx's visions of science in cahoots with industry have been wildly surpassed. Once upon a time, industry had its own "in-house" Research and Development (R&D) arm; now, it has universities, its off-site R&D arm. University science is little more than a handmaiden for big corporate business. Indeed, universities are themselves big corporate businesses and university research an external department of industry. Biotech, software, and pharmaceutical enterprises now cluster in and around major university campuses everywhere, blurring the boundary between scientific endeavor and capitalist commerce. The two are synonymous and the symbiosis is rarely questioned. It's just as Marx thought: "Invention becomes a branch of business, and the application of science to immediate production aims at determining the inventions at the same time as it solicits them."

Yet the business of science goes much further and much deeper than the university. It percolates through the whole fabric of our society, bringing a new kind of business ethic into our lives, especially into our cities, which now seem to be neo-capitalist factories for valorization. Technology might have once powered the assembly line, and in scattered global cases still does; but more widespread is its engineering of the "science of cities," with its own "unvarying regularity of the complex automaton." In the old factory, the capitalist formulated an autocratic power over workers; now, in cities, technology becomes the new overseer, helping keep cities as profitable as possible, filling in the financial pores not only of time but also of space, of exploitable urban space.

This new science of cities sees "smart" techno-cities as bright and fresh, vast isotropic planes and seamless webs of connectivity, where objects and entities circulate in a smooth, frictionless space, and where information flows and business flourishes. Such paradigms of urban life have been most energetically endorsed by big mainframe techie companies like Cisco Systems and IBM, as well as by engineering and consultancy giants such as AECOM and McKinsey. Their unanimous mission is to embed wireless broadband and computerized sensors into urban infrastructure everywhere.

Every piece of street furniture, from lampposts and traffic lights, to bike racks and domestic appliances and home heating systems will comprise the "Internet of Things," a global business niche said to be worth around 1.7 trillion dollars. Every credit card transaction, GPS usage, city street plan, subway and bus schedule, traffic flow pattern, graph of land and property prices, census tract, electricity consumption, etc.— all this and much more can be fed into a model out of which algorithmic averages emerge, calculating our future "optimal" city, how best it should be organized and governed. Though by whom rarely gets a mention.

Meanwhile, the enormous information database that ensues will be monetized by private capital in what may well be the most innovative development yet to extract relative surplus-value from the totality of daily life.

All this might be a new testing ground for Marx's ideas around technology and science, the context in which we should perhaps update him, reread him, think through some of his ideas. Nevertheless, there's one basic theme that remains timeless: technology, in its capitalist guise, always has been, always will be, an innovative method to discipline working people. It quite fundamentally revolutionizes the agency through which the capital relation is formally mediated, Marx says. Its deployment creates fear and division among workers and boosts production by bloating needless consumption. Conflict and dissent don't figure within its algorithms, either, nor do democratic debates about its implementation. Technology pleads innocence, experienced at masking the social power lying behind its control and manipulation.

11.

Marx is surprisingly quiet in chapter 15 about the role of class struggle. Toward the end, in Part 9 over several pages, he projects the immanent possibilities for a technologically driven society, one that functions around people's needs, varies the nature of their work, and even shortens the working day. But he hardly says anything about how we might reach that utopian point. Though he does give us a few hints of what he thinks *is not* required: "the whole-scale destruction of machinery which occurred in the English manufacturing districts during the first fifteen years of the nineteenth century, largely the result of the employment of the power-loom." Here, of course, Marx is referring to the Luddite movement, to the legendary machine-breakers rallying around their folkloric hero, Ned Ludd. "It took both time and experience," Marx says, "before the workers learnt to distinguish between machinery and its employment by capital, and therefore to transfer their attacks from the material instruments of production to the form of society which utilizes those instruments."

Marx distances himself from a rage against the machine. Since the Luddites, we've seen this rage unfold in both fiction and fact, from Joseph Conrad's *The Secret Agent*, where the mad anarchist Verloc wanted to blow up London's Greenwich Meridian, to the Unabomber's two-decade bombing spree, targeting everything and anyone in America involved in technological development. (Along the way, we could probably throw into the lot Al-Qaeda and, for that matter, the Book of Revelation.) But Marx's approach is more grown-up than wholesale rejection of new technology; it's more nuanced in its dialectic of ambiguity.

That's not to say there aren't problems with it, even if they're sometimes problems not of Marx's own choosing. For one thing, our current society, with its Twitter streams and tabloid soundbites—viscerally reducing social complexity to a few snappy buzzwords—makes it hard for a nuanced discussion, like Marx's, to get a satisfactory hearing. The other problem, however, is of Marx's making: it's not clear, for instance, what any nuanced action against an abstract and virtual technological system might these days entail.

Marx's point against the Luddites is well meant, but there's a sense, too, in which he underestimated the Luddites' anti-capitalist stance, giving short shrift to their ties to nascent trade unionism and to the growing workers' underground. Arguably, the Luddites offered a way into attacking not just the material instruments of production but also the form of society that utilized them. To that degree, their agitation and activism remains instructive, maybe even inspiring, in our own abrasively technocratic and technological age.

Much controversy, to say nothing of mystery, surrounds the Luddite movement, even down to whether Ned Ludd actually existed as a person. Some studies suggest the movement was a lot more sophisticated than it was cracked up to be. One of the best reinterpretations, pitched from a Marxist perspective, is E. P. Thompson's magisterial *The Making of the English Working Class* (1963), which sought to "rescue the Luddite cropper from the enormous condescension of posterity." Luddite attacks, says Thompson, had particular industrial objectives: "the destruction of power-looms (Lancashire), shearing-frames (Yorkshire), and resistance to the breakdown of custom in the Midlands framework-knitting industry." To explain these actions, he says, we need to look beyond immediate economic and industrial grievances.

When we do, Thompson reckons that the Luddites emerge as a tight-knit secret organization, a shadowy political movement that covered its tracks, left no minutes to its clandestine meetings, no written evidence of its activities, nothing to incriminate itself. Many activists and lawbreakers did end up on the scaffold. But, contrary to being a band of roughneck thugs, Thompson suggests, its members were well-informed about the laws of industry and trade unions. As a highly disciplined group of men and fellow-traveler women, their policy was nothing short of the "diffusion of agitation." Luddites were smart and skilled, privileged textile workers glaringly aware that they were undergoing a deterioration in status. "They were," Thompson says, "in direct conflict with the machinery which both they and their employers knew perfectly well would displace them."

And yet, at the same time, the character of Luddism wasn't blind protest. Nor was it operating narrowly, with immediate selfish, reactionary interests in mind. Indeed, Thompson argues that "Luddism was a quasi-insurrectionary movement which continually trembled on the edge of ulterior revolutionary objectives. This is not to say that it was a wholly conscious revolutionary movement; on the other hand, it had a tendency towards becoming such a movement, and it is this tendency which is most often understated." The Luddites were the first collective group to launch agitations that led to the Ten Hours' movement; and they called for an alternative political economy and morality to laissez-faire, to the irresponsible and unlicensed competition of the Industrial Revolution. What they instigated, all told, was an open-eyed class warfare.[19]

Perhaps the Luddite sensibility can be applied to our

own microchip age. Can we take a sledgehammer to the mainframe the same way the Luddites took it to the knitting-frame? Probably not. Likely Marx's more nuanced approach might come into its own, yet mixed with a healthy dose of Luddite skepticism, which pits itself against the pixel panopticon and business technocracy before us. Perhaps the Luddite equivalent nowadays is the call for disgruntled citizens to go off-grid? Or maybe we should mobilize the Luddites' insurrectionary character to start a class war with their weapons?

In his unsettling dystopian novel *The Circle* (2013), Dave Eggers reimagines what life would look like if an omnipotent tech company, the Circle, took over the world's governments and controlled every aspect of public and private life. Visualize a dream conglomerate of Google, Microsoft, Facebook, and Amazon headquartered in a dazzling California campus, where employees live and breathe the company and have no life beyond work. That's the picture. "Outside the walls of the Circle," someone says, "all was noise and struggle, failure and filth. But here, all had been perfected."

It's a reality that throws Marx's commodity fetishism back in people's faces, because now nothing is hidden anymore: all is transparent, trackable, observable, quantifiable. Embedded in every nook and cranny of life are millions of commercial "SeeChange" cameras, which can pan in and out on every big or little act on planet Earth, letting us glimpse precise details in the densest cities, on the tallest mountaintops, in melting glaciers and arid deserts. Nothing is private anymore. Not even going to the toilet. "All that happens will be known." The only thing that remains invisible is ideology, the market belief system implicit in the transparency.

One skeptical character, Mercer, isn't up for it. He knows it's a capitalist scam and wants out. But this is a big problem. Somehow, he is worse being offline than on, worse unplugging himself and fleeing than standing his ground and engaging. It's like sheltering under a tree during a lightning strike. He writes his ex-girlfriend Mae, the book's central protagonist, one last note. She's been bitten and smitten by the Circle and wants nothing else. She once loved Mercer but now hates his guts because he's a loser, a symbol of the mess outside, the past she wants to expunge. "By the time you read this, I'll be off the grid," Mercer tells his ex,

> and I expect that others will join me. In fact, I know others will join me. We'll be living underground, and in the desert, in the woods. We'll be like refugees, or hermits, some unfortunate but necessary combination of the two. Because this is what we are. I expect this is some second great schism, where two humanities will live, apart but parallel. There will be those who live under the surveillance dome you're helping to create, and those who live, or try to live, apart from it. I'm scared to death for us all.

He's right to be scared; fleeing in his pickup truck, SeeChange cameras track him and drones hunt him down. In fierce determination to get out, to escape beyond their gaze, Mercer ploughs his vehicle through a barrier and careens into a gorge—dead.

There's another skeptic in *The Circle*. He's an insider who's also an outsider. Wearing "an enormous hoodie," he looks like an occupier or Black bloc revolter, but he's none other than the Circle's boy-wonder visionary, Tyler Gospodinov, the company's first "Wise Man," whom everybody knows as Ty. Mae knows him as Kalden, Ty's alter ego, his shadow self, a kind of Edward Snowden whistleblower who warns her of the closing of the Circle, of the totalitarian nightmare he'd helped create.

He's not running away from anything—he's hacking it, trying to disassemble it from the inside. The other Wise Men, says Malden, have "professionalized our idealism, monetarized our utopia." They "saw the connection between our work and politics," he says, "and between politics and control. Public-private leads to private-private, and soon you have the Circle running most or even all government services, with incredible private-sector efficiency and an insatiable appetite." It sounds frighteningly familiar.

Kalden knows more than Mercer. He's not so much a great refuser as a double agent, maybe more Engels-like, calling out to others who aren't unplugged and offline but are tuned in, masters and mistresses of both worlds and who know the limitations of each. They know what's what, know how to strategize, how to disrupt. They know how resistance these days is more ontological than epistemological, something that cuts right inside you, into your beliefs and democratic hopes. It needs to be wholesale, a total way of being. "There used to be an option of opting out," Kalden says at the end of *The Circle*. "But now that's over . . . The Circle needs to be dismantled."

12.

Maybe we can think of computer hacker groups like "Anonymous" in this neo-Luddite vein, as digital dissenters and direct-action hacktivists who haunt the ghost in the machine. With an international reach, Anonymous has already unnerved the global financial and political powers that be. In November 2010, Julian Assange's WikiLeaks started to release thousands of diplomatic cables about US economic and military plans, its weapons systems, and initiatives against terrorism. The US government retaliated, kicking WikiLeaks off the server; PayPal, MasterCard, and Visa also pulled the plug. In response, with "Operation Avenge Assange," Anonymous hacked Paypal's website, bringing it down, and disrupted MasterCard's and Visa's. PayPal reputedly lost $5.5 million from the hijack. "WE ARE ANONYMOUS. WE ARE LEGION. WE DO NOT FORGIVE. WE DO NOT FORGET. EXPECT US."[20]

Anonymous's dark humor plays with Marxian ambiguity at the same time as it embraces the shtick of Dostoevsky and Kafka; the movement gets off on what it calls *lulz*, a deviant style that revels in demonic laughter and cyber infiltration of big organizations and big bureaucracies, targeting individuals within them, spreading humiliating information on corporate bigwigs and politicians who deserve to be humiliated, uploading videos on YouTube, generally creating mayhem with its cyberattacks and trickster campaigns. Anonymous seems representative of a newly forming, looser coterie of smart and concerned younger people. They span the entire globe, dialogue in many different languages, yet find their collective lingua franca in the growing array of informational technology acronyms like SMS, PDA, GPS, GPL, XML, etc.

Technology's prowess, Marx says, rests on its ability "to increase the productive power of the individual by means of cooperation," by creating a new productive power, "which is intrinsically a collective one." The problem with this form of cooperation is that it's phony; it is controlled exclusively by the bourgeoisie. It's a collective power, in other words, that's used to exploit social labor, not mobilize it cooperatively for the common good. But Marx's dialectic cuts both ways: this cooperative power, hastened as it is by globalization and information technology, opens up new potentialities for revolt and resistance. Marx knows it and so do groups like Anonymous. The "unavoidable antagonism," Marx says, is that "as the number of cooperative workers increases so too does their resistance to the domination of capital."

Marx imagines how a technologically advanced society could realize human needs and desires. If only technology could be wrested from private gain and put to cooperative public use. If only cooperation could lead to technology becoming a *common property* right rather than an Intellectual Property Right (IPR). This vision of cooperation is one of the most hopeful things dramatized in *Capital*, and it's there in chapter 15, lying undeveloped, in a raw, tentative state. Given all the miseries and horrors technology inflicts on working-class people, it's a miracle that Marx can pull us back from the brink. But he gives us an ideal of humanity that is rich

and expansive, generous in its affirmation of us as fundamentally cooperative beings—not ruthlessly competitive
animals involved in some war of all against all.

Much as Marx admired Darwin, he never accepted
human life as a competitive struggle. The admiration was
genuine enough; we've seen it already, expressed in footnote 4 to chapter 15, cuing the whole discussion on technology. In footnote 6 to chapter 14, on "The Division of
Labour," Marx had also called Darwin's *On the Origin of
Species* "an epoch-making work." Remember, too, these
were precisely the two chapters (14 and 15) that Marx
wanted to dedicate to Darwin. (Darwin, flattered, politely
declined.) But there's a possibility that Marx's intentions
might have also been laced with a certain irony and provo-
cation. Maybe Darwin recognized it.

Privately, Marx told Engels that it's "remarkable
how Darwin rediscovers, among the beasts and plants,
the society of England with its division of labour, competition, opening up of new markets, 'inventions' and
Malthusian 'struggle for existence.' It is Hobbes *bellum
omnium contra omnes*." Engels shared Marx's skepticism about Darwin: "The whole Darwinian theory of
the struggle for existence," he said, "is simply the trans-
ference from society to animate nature of Hobbes' theory
of the war of every man against every man and the bourgeois theory of competition, along with the Malthusian
theory of population."

Darwin's biggest stumbling block, for Marx, was
Malthus, the English parson-cum-political economist,
the prophet of a quack theory of overpopulation. Tolstoy
had cut to the chase, calling Malthus a "malicious

mediocrity." Why, then, had Darwin so uncritically accepted Malthus's bourgeois claptrap? Perhaps because Darwin *was* bourgeois? Perhaps because he had married into a bourgeois industrialist's family? Emma, Darwin's wife (and first cousin), was the daughter of Josiah Wedgwood, the prominent Staffordshire pottery mogul. And father-in-law Josiah was credited with industrializing pottery manufacture, intensifying divisions of labor, and trimming labor costs at his factories—all of which helped his empire expand throughout the world. Competition and divisions of labor were evidently "virtues" in the family's blood. (So, too, apparently, was child labor: in footnote 82 of "The Working Day," Marx notes how, in 1863, twenty-six firms owning extensive potteries in Staffordshire, including Josiah Wedgwood & Sons, presented a petition saying that competition with other capitalists didn't allow them to voluntarily limit the hours worked by children.)

Darwin's theory of natural selection took from Malthus the belief that population growth would outrun food supply. The result is an overt battle for dwindling resources. The world is here seen crowded out by species jostling each other for survival. It's so packed that only by shoving out another inhabitant can a new species live. Darwin used the metaphor of the "wedge" to highlight how any new species literally had to wedge themselves into another, creating their own little chink by forcing the other out. Success came from bullying out a rival, making space for oneself at their expense. It's hard to get a better description of bourgeois political economy in action, as well as the reactionary little Englander mentality, in which immigrants are the new wedges trying to chip away scarce homegrown resources.

Marx had another kind of humanity in mind: "When the worker cooperates in a planned way with others, he strips off the fetters of his individuality and develops the capabilities of his species." Implicit in this understanding is that cooperation enables our species to flourish. It is only through cooperation that individuals can develop a fuller sense of individuality, as well as a "higher form" of coexistence. In fact, even in Marx's time there were other visions of evolutionary theory that emerged outside bourgeois England. If social Darwinism seemed internalized in nineteenth-century British social and economic life, this wasn't the case in Russia, where Darwin's evolutionary theory was most categorically questioned.

Russia was a vast, sparsely populated land, most of its giant territory harsh, barren, and cold. Life here might have been nasty, brutish, and short but it wasn't because of any principle of overpopulation, or straining of potential supplies of food and space. Too many people with too few resources? This would have seemed an utterly absurd conception for any Russian. In other words, Darwin's Malthusian underpinnings weren't quite as universally applicable as the great scientist might have thought. Wasn't Darwin merely projecting onto the natural world a particular ideology about competitive open markets in his own crowded social world? Wasn't Darwin just following Malthus as an article of bourgeois faith?

Such was the belief of Peter Kropotkin, the Russian anarchist prince, geographer, and geologist, and author of numerous heterodox texts, including *Mutual Aid*

(1902). The work, written in English in Bromley, Kent (Darwin's own county), bore a revealing subtitle: "*A Factor of Evolution.*" Kropotkin says at the beginning of his inquiry how two aspects of animal life impressed him most during his long travels around eastern Siberia and northern Manchuria. One was the extreme severity of the environment and the desperate struggle for existence most species had to wage there. The second was that "even when animal life teemed in abundance," Kropotkin says, "I failed to find the bitter struggle for the means of existence." During heavy snowstorms, across miles and miles of iced-up tundra, amid howling winds and Arctic temperatures, "in all the scenes of animal life which passed before my eyes, I saw mutual aid and mutual support carried on to the extent which made me suspect in it a feature of the greatest importance for the maintenance of life, the preservation of each species, and its further evolution." If animals and insects fought one another in this brutal environment, they'd have wiped each other out long ago.

Maybe if Darwin had traveled to chilly, empty Siberia, rather than to a fecund tropics, with its superabundant plant and animal life, another image of nature might have emerged. If, Kropotkin wonders, "we ask, 'who are the fittest: those who are continually at war with each other, or those who support one another?' we at once see that those animals which acquire habits of mutual aid are undoubtedly the fittest. They have more chances to survive, and they attain, in their respective classes, the highest development of intelligence and bodily organization." Kropotkin yearned to import these natural laws into the laws of government and community life. Self-sustaining, cooperative societies could become the conditioning laws of human culture, he thought, life-forms based on solidarity and peace rather than competition and slaughter. "The unsociable species," he concluded, throwing the gauntlet down today, "are doomed to decay."[21]

We have no record of Marx and Kropotkin ever meeting. Most likely they never did. They would have probably treated each other with suspicion even if they had. And yet, notwithstanding their doctrinal disagreements, Marx's evolutionary theory of "the productive organs of man in society" ends up being a lot closer to Kropotkin's than to Darwin's. If anything, "mutual aid" marks the dénouement of chapter 15, the means through which capitalist production "can be dissolved and then reconstructed on a new basis." Bleak Siberia appears the more meaningful metaphor for the English labor system than does a tropical paradise overflowing with warm life. In the former domain, survival necessitates creatures working together in cooperation, collectively bargaining, and forging some associative mutuality of the oppressed to ward off extinction.

Marx closes chapter 15 with a call for a new "collective working group," which, he says, will be "composed of individuals of both sexes," who, in unison, turn production "into a source of humane development." He even envisions the founding of socialist schools for the vocational teaching of technology, "where the children of workers receive a certain amount of instruction in technology and in the practical handling of the various implements of labor." It's a fascinating glimpse of Marx's educational system, influenced by Rousseau's *Emile* and the German progressive educational theorist J. B. Basedow. Primary schools would have children develop their intelligence by coming into closer contact with reality through practical activities. "Technological education," says Marx, "both theoretical and practical, will take its proper place in the schools of workers."

Yet to get that far,

> the possibility of varying labour must become a general law of social production, and the existing relations must be adapted to permit its realization in practice. That monstrosity, the disposable working population held in reserve, in misery, for the changing requirement of capitalist exploitation, must be replaced by the individual who is absolutely available for different kinds of labour; the partially developed individual, who is merely the bearer of one specialized social function, must be replaced by the totally developed individual, for whom the different social functions are different modes of activity they take in turn.

The latent possibility for varying labor, for making it fulfilling and authentic, is real enough for sensible people to see. Technology can take the stresses out of work, can shorten the working day, can create abundance for anyone, liberate people from drudgery, provide more free time for intellectual and artistic nourishment. It can transform the "partially developed individual," the bearer of one detail or de-skilled social function, into a "totally developed individual." This, then, is Marx's romantic dream: a society that breaks free of the vicious competitive circle of undefined productivity, of productivity for productivity's sake, of accumulation for the sake of capital accumulation.

Marx wrote *Capital* as a manifesto on how capitalism generalizes both overemployment and unemployment, being at once hypertrophic and atrophic. He warned of the progressive production of a "relative surplus population" who float in and out of jobs and whose destiny is entirely contingent on the whims of the business cycle. Yet, at the same time, as a dialectical counterflow, Marx also penned passages with daring leaps of the utopian imagination. Even in this dire system, he says, immanent possibilities reside for a planet that's been transformed into a vast arena of fixed capital. More than a hundred and fifty years on, Marx's reality is here, now.

He sees a world that "suspends living labour," that revolves around "dead labour," that organizes production around automation and high technology, as a society equipped with all the vital powers to reduce "necessary labour time." All the instruments are available, all the wherewithal is here for creating socially disposable time, for reducing labor time to a bare minimum, for freeing up everybody's time to engage in a more passionate and fulfilling life in and beyond work. It's a logic that requires us to embrace contradictions, to flow in Marx's counterflow. When the world is dominated by machines, when we've become appendages to machines, to new technology, then and seemingly only then, he thinks, are we on the verge of something new and possible. We've been on that verge for a while.

13.

If someone were to ask me what my favorite bit of Marx's *Capital* is, I'd tell them chapter 25, on "The General Law of Capitalist Accumulation." Not that anybody has ever asked me; but I suspect I wouldn't be alone in selecting this pinnacle performance, the beginning of the climactic unfurling of Volume One. For here those "laws of motion" that Marx had been trying to lay bare throughout *Capital* really do motor before the reader's very eyes, in all their disturbing fluidity. Hitherto, Marx had been attempting to piece together the intricate "inner mechanisms" of capitalist society. By chapter 25, he's ready to analyze these inner mechanisms as a giant, whirring machine.

And he's mesmerized by the prodigious power of this machine, of capital accumulating, bursting through every historical and geographical restriction, conquering the entire world of social wealth. At the same time, he's appalled by the ruthless force it unleashes and by the horrors the machine inflicts upon its cogs. Meanwhile, its normal functioning soon takes on a spiraling dynamic all its own, operating beyond the control of any single capitalist master. After a while, the enviable freedom of the capitalist gets transformed into a die-hard necessity, into an infamous historical mission: "Accumulation for accumulation's sake, production for production's sake."

The drive to accumulate capital dramatically pits capitalist against capitalist, capitalist against worker, worker against worker. Accumulation fuels competition, and competition, Marx says, "subordinates every individual capitalist to the immanent laws of capitalist production, as external, coercive laws." Thus, as capitalists strive to accumulate, as their actions become mere functions of capital, they inevitably clash with other capitalists seeking to do likewise. What erupts is a fratricidal war; different fractions of capital jostle one another, struggle to corner markets, to control and monopolize labor; a zero-sum accumulation mania transpires. Accumulation is the centrifugal impetus of "capital in general." But competition hastens a splintering of capital, just as it hastens a splintering of labor, compounding each side into many "aliquot parts." Thus, as capital accumulates, the formation and intensification of class structure manifests itself as a paradoxical obliteration of class structure.

Before long, the hullabaloo of accumulation is "supplemented" by concentration and centralization, by big capitalist fishes gobbling up little fishes and sharks chomping on the big fishes. Marx says this enhances the scale of operations, accelerates the overall effects of accumulation, but in uneven ways, for capitalists and workers alike. For, on the one hand, competition and the obligatory development of a credit system become powerful levers of centralization—of the formation of joint-stock companies, trusts and conglomerates, mergers and acquisitions—and of expanded accumulation. On the other hand, though, the "organic composition of capital"—the ratio of dead to living labor, of machines to workers, of constant to variable capital—gradually starts to creep upward, diminishing the relative demand for labor.

The system soon breeds a new species. Marx labels them "a new financial aristocracy, a new variety of parasites in the shape of promoters, speculators and nominal directors, a whole system of swindling and cheating by means of corporation promotion, stock issuance, and stock speculation." Could Marx be talking about us? By God yes. Nowadays, we know these people by name, by sleazy reputation; we know, too, that within the overall accumulation process this new financial aristocracy has a stake very different from that of productive capital's.

The former plays an extremely limited enabling role, if any, for valorization: stock exchanges are now billion-dollar markets for speculating on already existing stocks and shares. Little activity actually raises money for new productive investment. Businesses generate money by selling stock and shares, relinquishing part of the company to shareholders, but little of the accruing booty gets recycled into future investment. Invariably, it's doled out as dividends, and/or creamed off through inflated CEO salaries.

One of the reasons I like to affirm chapter 25 isn't only because it explains the working conditions of the world's peoples today: it also explains the conditions of our whole existence. Marx's General Law of Capitalist Accumulation is nothing less than the lever upon which all our lives now pivot. Its frame of reference needs to be opened out, onto the broader canvas of life, especially planetary urban life. The mighty machine has made us cogs everywhere. It's here where I'd like to develop Marx's law, "a law of tendency," as he calls it, which expels people from dwelling space as well as from the workplace. As such, this law isn't just a condition of earning a living; it's a condition of earning a life.

Marx knew in the 1860s that "the absolute" general law of capitalist accumulation could be "modified in its workings by many circumstances." But in every case, he says, it "followed that in proportion as capital accumulates, the situation of the worker, be their payment high or low, must grow worse." In our present-day neoliberal context, the economy flourishes through under- and over-employed workers: from Uber to Deliveroo, Handy to Hermes, Amazon to adjunct professors, work is evermore casualized and irregular; and worker benefits seem to diminish by the day. Toilers here assume that category Marx reckons the general law of capitalist accumulation progressively produces: "a relative surplus population"—or, alternatively, "an industrial reserve army of labor."

"Every worker," Marx believes, "belongs to this relative surplus population during the time when they are only partially or wholly employed." Marx, it's worth pointing out, sees *all* work under capitalism as precarious—always has been, always will be. It's a precariousness dependent on a consistently fickle capitalist business cycle, on short-term soars and long-haul dips. Wage levels, he says, are regulated by the expansion and contraction of the relative surplus population. Wages "aren't determined by the variations of the absolute numbers of the working population," Marx insists, "but by the varying proportions in which the working class is divided into an active army and reserve army, by the increase or diminution in the relative amount of surplus population, by the extent to which it is alternately absorbed and set free."

Sometimes wages might even rise should demand for labor rise. At these moments, wages can conceivably keep increasing so long as they don't impinge upon the overall expansion of capital. Something resembling this actually occurred during the boom of the 1950s and 1960s, when workers' real wages did in fact rise. Still, the more typical rule, Marx says, is that "the mechanism of capitalist production takes care that the absolute increase of capital isn't accompanied by a corresponding rise in the general demand for labour." Capital does something more innovative instead, something more dialectical. It "acts on both sides at once":

> If its accumulation on the one hand increases the demand for labour, it increases on the other the supply of workers by "setting them free," while at the same time the pressure of the unemployed compels those who are employed to furnish more labour, and therefore makes the supply of labour to a certain extent independent of the supply of workers. The movement of the law of supply and demand for labour on this basis completes the despotism of capital.

And under this despotism, real wages have effectively stagnated, almost nowhere keeping pace with cost-of-living hikes. One of the United States' top capitalist mouthpieces, the *Harvard Business Review*, admits that inflation-adjusted hourly wages for the typical American worker have, since the early 1970s, hardly risen, edging upward a mere 0.2 percent per year. Throughout this period, remember, the overall economy has been growing. Thus American workers haven't participated in any of the growth nor benefited from gains in their own pro-ductivity. The reason why is classic Volume One: new technology has put downward pressure on less skilled workers' wages; and workers displaced from employ-ment send disciplinary messages to those still active in work: *Work harder or else!*

Whether in times of prosperity or decline, the indus-trial reserve army produces much the same effect. "It weighs down the active army of workers; during periods of over-production and feverish activity, it puts a curb on their pretensions." The relative surplus population is "the background against which the law of the demand and supply of labour does its work. It confines the field of action of this law to the limits absolutely convenient to capital's drive to exploit and dominate workers."

If we dig a little deeper into chapter 25, we can see how Marx identifies three types of relative surplus popu-lation: stagnant, floating, and latent. Alas, we don't need to dig too deeply to see how Marx's types remain our types. The stagnant form, for a start, is "part of the active labour army," he says, "but with extremely irregular employment. Hence it offers capital an inexhaustible res-ervoir of disposable labour-power." It's characterized "by a maximum of working time and a minimum of wages." The downsized blue-collar worker might be filed under this category, since stagnant surplus populations, Marx says, are "recruited from workers in large-scale industry who have become redundant, and especially from decay-ing branches of industry where handicraft is giving way to manufacture, and manufacture to machinery."

This stagnant workforce consists of time-served men

repulsed from blue-collar employment and drawn into irregular jobs like security guards, janitors, cabbies, and deliverymen. Older generation blue-collar workers, who once worked the mines, the auto plants, and steel mills, now find themselves literally stagnant. They're no longer able (or willing) to do low-grade work, yet are too young to retire. So instead they slouch into the ranks of a non-participating labor force. Men who once set rivets together now sit alone, able to recite daytime TV schedules by heart. Utter stagnation lingers everywhere in Rust Belt Europe and America, where empty union halls look out over the rubble of what used to be the company plant.

The dialectic of the floating relative surplus population is similarly one of repulsion and attraction, but its charge is much more volatile. Participants here encounter working conditions wholly unstable and uncertain. The only thing that's regular is the irregularity of their work. These men and women represent a huge pool of underemployed and sub-employed workers: part-time, on-call, self-employed or zero-hours contractors (the employer is not obligated to provide a minimum number of hours), whose résumés are marked by a floating in and out of jobs. Despite the job-hopping, few new skills are ever learned. Steadily, its fluctuating force assumes a predictably deadening life-form.

Many workers are absorbed into the "personnel services industry," where the hiring and firing is managed by employment agencies like ManpowerGroup, which recruits temporary workers across America and the world. (Manpower has offices in fifty countries, and places 1.6

million "in assignments with more than 250,000 businesses worldwide annually . . . providing our customers
with productive workers and our employees with work.")
The growth of this personnel services industry means
ever more despotic control of an anarchic labor market.
Supply and demand for labor tightly track the expansions
and contractions of capital; yet always its motioning seeks
to trim monies laid out on variable capital.

As of May 2017, the U.S. Bureau of Labor Statistics
said nearly 6 million workers are "contingent," that is,
"persons who do not expect their jobs to last or who
report that their jobs are temporary." Moreover, there are
a further 10.6 million people working as "independent
contractors," together with another 2.6 million on-call.
And this doesn't include 1.4 million temporary help
workers nor the 933,000 employed by contract firms
like Manpower. Which suggests that true numbers for
contingent America tot up to somewhere in the region
of 20 million people. No coincidence that the nation's
two largest employers are contingent kings Walmart and
McDonald's.[22]

Tech giants like Google, often seen as egalitarian
employers with idyllic workplaces, are likewise massive-
ly reliant on temporary and contracted labor. In fact, "a
shadow workforce of temps" now outnumber Google's
full-time employees. As of March 2019, Google uses
121,000 temp and contracted workers, compared with
a full-time workforce of 102,000. Google temps are
employed by outside agencies and, in the United States,
make less money than Google full-timers. They have different benefits packages and no paid vacation. Last April,

hundreds of Google employees signed a letter protesting the company's "two-tier system," as well as the dismissal of 80 percent of a 43-person artificial intelligence team of contingent workers. OnContracting, a temp employment agency for the high-tech industry, says that companies like Google save $100,000 a year on average per American job by using a temporary contractor instead of a full-time employee.[23]

Women swell the ranks of this floating contingent workforce. In the United States, women are three times as likely to hold regular and irregular part-time work as men. These women make up about a fifth of the overall female workforce, earning, on average, 20 percent less than equivalent women employed full-time and 20 percent less than their male counterpart part-timers. Minority groups fare worse than their Anglo peers, and minority women worst of all. On the whole, African American women tend to be twice as likely to be lower-paid temps and much less likely to be self-employed; Hispanic women, meanwhile, represent a larger share of low-wage on-call work.

Capitalism has a handy knack of constantly inventing and reinventing its reserve army of labor. Often it does so miraculously, tapping into assorted branches of society and sectors of industry where labor has been lying *latent*. Thus, alongside the stagnant and floating forms, Marx acknowledges another category of flexible labor, the "latent" category, a sort of reserve reserve army of laborers. "As soon as capitalist production takes possession of agriculture," he says, "and in proportion to the extent to which it does so, the demand for a rural working population falls absolutely."

Part of the agricultural population is therefore constantly on the point of passing over into an urban population or manufacturing proletariat. There is a constant flow from this source of the relative surplus population. But the constant movement towards towns presupposes, in the countryside itself, a constant latent surplus population.

The movement of peoples from rural to urban areas, from agriculture to a city-based factory system, continued apace during the twentieth-century. As of 2006, its flow tipped the global demographic balance: the majority of the world's inhabitants, some 3.3 billion people, live in urban agglomerations, not rural areas. Some of that generation's latent surplus populations— people formerly displaced from agriculture and reabsorbed into urban factories—have since fallen into the ranks of floating and stagnant relative surplus urban populations. By 2030, 60 percent of the world's population is projected to be urban; an additional 590,000 square miles of the planet will be urbanized, a land surface more than twice the size of Texas, spelling an additional 1.47 billion city dwellers, many of whom will bolster the ranks of a latent reserve army. They'll offer sustained nourishment for expanded capitalist accumulation everywhere.

A big chunk of this latent surplus population lurks in China. Shanghai is the planet's fastest growing metropolis, expanding a massive 15 percent each year since 1992, boosted by $120 billion of foreign direct investment. Half the world's cranes are reputed to be working in Shanghai's Pudong district. Rice paddies have been filled with modern skyscrapers and vast factories. Outlying farm-lands now host the world's fastest train links and the tallest hotel. Four thousand buildings with twenty or more stories have gone up, ensuring Shanghai has twice the number of buildings as New York. With 171 cities of more than one million inhabitants each, China over the past decade has commandeered nearly half the world's cement supplies, and it will doubtless monopolize the world's supply and demand for latent surplus labor populations.

Of course, after 1989, with the tumbling of the Berlin Wall, another reservoir of latent labor flooded the capital-ist marketplace. A freshly proletarianized workforce ini-tiated a new round of primitive accumulation of capital, transforming former Eastern European state employees into freelance wage-laborers, set free to pit their wits on the flexible European labor market. The Eastern Bloc's headlong embrace of Western-style neoliberalism prised open a whole new array of market niches, together with a latent labor reserve—both at home, in some newly formed nation-states, and in the European Economic Area (EEA). Almost overnight an ideology of dictatorial personality morphed into an ideological dictatorship of the free mar-ket, with its attendant rights of consumerist man.

Out of the ashes of communism rose the Phoenix of cheap labor. Western manufacturers, halving labor costs, beat a hasty path eastward while a lot of latent labor, almost as hastily, trekked westward. Stimulated by the European Union's freedom of labor movement, they've found low-grade jobs in powerhouses like Brit-ain, Germany, and France. Pay is better than before, yet much less than that of homegrown workers. British businesses have prospered enormously from this influx of Eastern European labor, especially Polish. Enterprises have been able to valorize a cheap labor they'd not had since the 1950s, when Afro-Caribbean immigrants arrived. The British agricultural sector has been a big gainer. Prior to 2004, crops like asparagus, cherries, raspberries, and strawberries were suffering long-term decline. Remuneration in these sectors was meager and the work backbreaking. Few locals were turned on. Yet since 2004, rather than invest in expensive new berry-picking technology, growers have exploited Eastern European labor reserves; latent labor-power has rekindled agricultural capital accumulation and boosted productivity.

14.

When Marx formulated his General Law of Capitalist Accumulation, cities were sites for manufacturing valorization. It was in the urban factories where commodities got produced and surplus-value created. The factory system—"Modern Industry," Marx called it—was the mainstay of capital accumulation, and workers were attracted and repelled from this urban employment. In chapter 25, however, Marx notes how the general law operates outside the factory gates as well, vividly exemplified, he says, in " 'improvements' of towns which accompany the increase in wealth, such as the demolition of badly built districts, the erection of palaces to house banks, warehouses, etc., the widening of streets for business traffic, for luxury carriages, for the introduction of tramways, [which] obviously drive the poor away into even worse and more crowded corners."

It's not a bad description of what still happens in big cities today. Marx's point here is that "the greater the centralization of the means of production, the greater is the corresponding concentration of workers within a given space; and therefore the more quickly capitalist accumulation takes place, the more miserable the housing situation of the working class." Landlords squeeze workers, ripping them off at home, as tenants, just as industrialists rip them off at work, as wage-laborers. Rents are high precisely because pay is low. Vulnerable workers equate to vulnerable tenants; both feel the force of "property and its rights."

"Everyone knows," Marx says, "that the dearness of houses stands in inverse ratio to their quality, and that these mines of misery are exploited by house speculators with more profit and less cost than the mines of Potosi were ever exploited. The antagonistic character of capitalist accumulation, and thus of capitalist property-relations in general, is here so evident." Marx's adopted hometown of London, one of the world's richest cities, had the most squalid, overcrowded habitations, "absolutely unfit for human beings." Marx knew this because he and his family lived in many of these hovels. "Rents have become so heavy," he cites one government health inspector saying, "that few labouring men can afford more than one room." (1865 or 2020?)

And yet, in another sense, plenty has changed since Marx's day. Back then, his focus was on production *in* the industrial city; a century and a half on, the city itself has become the form of industrialization. In the 1860s, cities were places where commodities got produced; nowadays, *cities are themselves commodities*, centers of gravity for the General Law of Capitalist Accumulation and for the expansive power of capital. Now, urban space itself is both the subject and object of valorization, the means of production as well as the product this means of production creates. In manufacturing, Marx said, new technology would prompt a change in the "organic composition of capital." "The growth in the mass of means of production," he argued, "as compared with the mass of labour-power that vivifies them, is reflected in its value-composition by the increase of the constant constituent of capital at the expense of its variable constituent."

So, too, now is the organic composition of capital in cities rising—quite literally rising. Constant capital is displacing variable capital: capital circulates into the construction of new fixed capital assets, new items of the built environment, such as office blocks and shopping malls, upscale housing and elite cultural amenities—high-yield activities for the expanded reproduction of capital rather than low-yield necessities for the simple reproduction of labor-power. This is the sense in which workers have now been set free from life, not just from work—they're displaced from dwelling space as they're rendered superfluous from the workplace.

One of the biggest jamborees of urban capitalist accumulation these days comes from New York City: Hudson Yards. In the spring of 2019, I was in New York and did a big walk around the Hudson Yards development with my friend and former teacher, the Marxist theorist

David Harvey. It was a chilly, soaking wet afternoon, and we both tried our utmost not to let the weather, nor the awfulness of this project, a spillover from Michael Bloomberg's mayoral years, dampen our spirits.

The 12-acre site, west of Penn Station and Madison Square Garden, had once been gritty rail tracks and storage yards for Long Island Rail Road trains. Now, a $20 billion mega-plan promises shingled blue-glass skyscrapers, with office space, deluxe condos and high-end retailing galore, to say nothing of an eco arts center and bizarre pedestrian walkway. Completion isn't destined until 2024; but much is already in place. Hooking up to the High Line and a revamped No. 7 subway station, Hudson Yards is set to symbolize the pride and joy of a post-9/11 Big Apple, a celebration of Michael Bloomberg's bleeding edge: New York, Inc.

The bourgeoisie has torn away sentimental veils, Marx said in the *Communist Manifesto*, and put in its stead "open, shameless, direct, bare exploitation." In all this, Hudson Yards is built on familiar ground. The *New York Times* architecture critic, Michael Kimmelman, called the development "a super-sized suburban-style office park, with a shopping mall and a quasi-gated condo community targeted at the 0.1%." It's the largest private real estate venture in US history, and as the brazen world leader of private real estate deals that's saying a great deal.

In office, Bloomberg pumped 75 million public dollars into the development, matching it with a similar sum from his own deep pockets. BlackRock, meantime, a midtown investment company, managing a $6 trillion portfolio, wrote off $25 million in state tax credits, buff-ering the move of its 700-person workforce to Hudson Yards, less than a mile westward. Some estimates suggest the whole initiative has totaled as much as $6 billion in tax breaks and public finding. Socialism for billionaires is how the scam has been described—even as those self-same scammers wax lyrical about the virtues of the "free market."

Still, one of the most startling of the Hudson Yards scams, reputed to have amassed some $1.6 billion's worth of financing, is even more insidious, only recently becoming public news.[24] It centers on the controversial investor visa program called EB-5, part of George H. W. Bush's immigration reform of the early 1990s. Bizarre as it may sound, the program lets immigrants secure visas in exchange for investment in the U.S. economy. We're talking here about the super-rich, people who can pump between $500K and a million bucks into American real estate. That will enable them—no questions asked, no hoop-jumping—to gain fast-track visas, for work or study (EB-5 has been something of a favorite in recent years among wealthy Chinese families). The monies are meant to go into poor and distressed neighborhoods across America, so-called TEAs—Targeted Employment Areas.

But the jurisdiction of TEAs—where its boundary lines are drawn—is rather loose, hence open to meddling and manipulation. In New York, Empire State Develop-ment, a public-private organization under the state gov-ernment's banner, is the arch-meddler and manipulator. Somehow, it managed to secure Hudson Yards TEA sta-tus, stretching its remit into poor census tracks of Harlem.

Thus funds intended for real estate aid in poverty-stricken neighborhoods, such as Harlem, were siphoned off and redirected into a super-luxury mega-development. "Think of it as a form of creative financial gerrymandering," is how Kriston Capps put it. That's how developer Related Companies raked in around $380 million at Hudson Yards, bypassing distressed area scrutiny through a greedy audacity that beggars belief. Or perhaps not, in Trump's America. (And by the way, son-in-law Jared Kushner has been busily promoting Kushner Companies' projects with EB-5 investors in China.)

Something more publicly obvious at Hudson Yards is, however, the scale of its banality. A stroll around doesn't reveal too much intrigue. What we find here is something not only unfair but uninteresting, a city space flattened by familiarity, even as those glitzy skyscrapers go up. It's the sort of predictability that only money can buy. Its ubiquity resides in its sameness, in the predictability of both its form and function. Here, as elsewhere, we have the same predictable city within a city, the same sleek glass and steel architectural structures, housing the same financial and high-tech services, the same multinational corporations and accountancy firms, same banks and management consultancies, same retail giants destined for the same wealthy consumers. In the mix, there's no mix. All real urban texturing is expunged.

Apart from, that is, a mix of spectacular gimmickry. First off, we have the "Vessel," touted as Manhattan's Eiffel Tower, designed by Brit Thomas Heatherwick, a $200 million 16-story pedestrian walkway, a stairway to nowhere, looking like a truncated giant honeycomb, serving no other purpose than to serve, than to promote spectacular contemplation.

Nearby comes the "Shed," a $500 million eco-friendly arts center and performance space, which actually looks like a shed, or, as someone said, like an aircraft hangar wrapped in a down comforter. Maybe it's a quilted Chanel handbag. At any rate, the structure is a movable feast, a shell that glides along rails, seating 1,200 people at any one time, "physically transforming itself," the hype says, "to support artists' most ambitious ideas." Which artists? Whose ambitious ideas? We still have to see. In 2013, the City of New York handed over $50 million toward the project, to Related Companies and the Oxford Properties Group, representing the single biggest capital grant given in that year.

Wandering around Hudson Yards, David and I spoke of "the restless analyst," something he'd written about over thirty years ago, in his book *Consciousness and the Urban Experience*. It's the mythical figure haunting *The American Scene* (1907), Henry James's roving travelogue around fin-de-siècle America. James had been away from the United States for twenty-five years, living in Europe. As a "returning absentee," he spent 1904–1905 rediscovering his native land, indignant at much he saw. Many changes, he said, became "a perpetual source of irritation." "Charming places, charming objects," James wrote, "languish all around the restless analyst, under designations that seem to leave the smudge of a great vulgar thumb."

The gaze of James's restless analyst was the gaze of "an inquiring stranger." The character likely came to mind at Hudson Yards because we, too, felt like "inquiring strangers," out of place and similarly indignant at much we saw. In *Consciousness and the Urban Experience*, David said he'd "long been impressed with this character the restless analyst. It seems to capture the only kind of intellectual stance possible in the face of a capitalism that reduces all aspects of social, cultural, and political (to say nothing of economic) life to the pure homogeneity and universality of money values and then transforms them according to the roving calculus of profit." It's hard to better this as an insight into what was unfolding all around us.

Maybe the restless analyst can be a sort of radical archetype, somebody we need more than ever today, an "inquiring stranger" who scours the capitalist landscape, restlessly keeping abreast of capitalism's reckless penchant for melting things into air, leveling everything even as it builds up. Perhaps the restless analyst is the archetypal modern commentator, whose skeptical gaze is never seduced by dazzling appearances, by that smudge of capitalism's great vulgar thumb.

When it comes to the "roving calculus of profit" in cities nowadays, the question of land rent has to be foremost on any restless analyst's mind. Marx, that most restless of restless analysts, didn't actually say much about urban land markets. His was a theory of agricultural groundrent where the central challenge lay in understanding how land can have a value without being a product of labor. In *The Limits to Capital*, David's masterpiece from 1982, urban land markets are tackled full on, and a brilliant reinterpretation of Marx's theory is offered. It's one of the book's most strikingly original features, a piece of genius in its apparent simplicity: that land under capitalism—especially urban land—has become another form of fictitious capital, another financial asset, having more in common with an asset-bearing investment—and hence with interest-bearing capital—than any arcane debate about rural soil fertility.

Ground rent is a kind of "imaginary capital," David said. "What is bought and sold is not the land, but title to the ground-rent yielded by it. The money laid out is equivalent to an interest-bearing investment. The buyer acquires a claim upon anticipated future revenues, a claim upon the future fruits of labour." So the "value of land" is intimately related to the circulation of interest-bearing capital, as well as to the stock market, and to finance capital in general. In this way the spatial landscape of cities is shaped by shifts in interest rates and by the ebbing and flowing of money capital. Perceptions of future rents deeply affect present land values and property prices. This speculative bent can make or break certain locations, conditioning what might, and might not, be built at any given moment. The built environment of cities thereby sways to the rhythm of capital accumulation.

In actuality, this notion isn't too far removed from Marx's understanding; he'd hinted as much in drafts of Volume Three of *Capital*. "In cities that are experiencing rapid growth," he said, "particularly where building is carried on with industrial methods, as in London, it is the *ground-rent* and not the *house* that forms the real object of speculation" (Marx's emphases). And elsewhere: "Capitalized ground-rent presents the appearance of the price of the value of land, so that the earth is bought and sold just like any other commodity."

Curiously, the recent publication of *Marx's Economic Manuscript of 1864–1865*, which made available for the first time the only full draft of Volume Three of *Capital*, has shone light on Marx's own view of ground rent.[25] I say Marx's "own view" here because the posthumous publication of Volume Three bore the heavy imprint of Engels, Marx's collaborator, who had edited and added, divided and subdivided, what Marx wrote as a continuous interconnected flow; the sections on interest-bearing capital and ground rent particularly suffered under Engels's stewardship. The former he blanketed with an overriding (and erroneous) concern for the "credit system"; the latter discussion on rent he chopped up and reordered into discrete sections. The reordering, alas, severed Marx's close affiliation between interest-bearing capital and ground rent—vindicating just how Marxian David's vision of rent actually is in *Limits to Capital*.

In the *Economic Manuscript of 1864–1865*, Marx called interest-bearing capital "the externalization of surplus-value." In interest-bearing capital, he said, "the capital relation reaches its most fetishized form." Here we have the appearance of money breeding money, money that no longer bears any trace of its origin. "The social relation is consummated in the relationship of a thing (money) to itself." It's clear how Marx viewed ground rent as another form of "externalized surplus-value," as something parasitic rather than productive, a redistribution of total surplus-value and hence a filching of the fruits of labor. Only, of course, it doesn't look like that.

Somebody has to pay, always; and usually it's the working classes who get fleeced with increased levels of exploitation and oppression. "The tremendous power this gives to landed property," said Marx, "when it is combined together with industrial capital in the same hands enables capital practically to exclude workers engaged in a struggle over wages from the very earth itself as a dwelling place." In a single sentence, Marx seems to have laid bare the whole dynamics of New York's housing and labor market. He added, immediately thereafter, in parentheses: "Here one section of society demands a tribute from the other for the right to inhabit the earth, just as in landed property in general the proprietors demand the right to exploit the earth's surface."

Interest-bearing capital circulates through land markets, chasing enhanced future ground rents; land prices get fixed accordingly. In a certain sense, the process becomes self-fulfilling: the pursuit of enhanced rents will often enhance those rents. Marketing, publicity, and "place-making" play their role. Exchange values are gouged out of what should be use values. Locations like Hudson Yards are preeminent expressions of capital becoming an automatic fetish. Space becomes an exploitable commodity, a monopolizable financial asset, a frackable parcel of planet Earth. Maximizing rent is akin to power-drilling for oil. Black gold in the city.

Yet the limits of capital's gyrations in the city might well be set by capital itself, by its own cannibalization of urban space. Aren't there endemic problems with expelling workers "from inhabiting the earth as a dwelling place"? They're value producers, after all. Won't capital here fall foul of its own automatic fetish, of money creating more money *ex nihilo*? Won't the limits to the General Law of Capitalist Accumulation really be the limits of the law's inherent logic?

This law creates a relative surplus population who feel the brunt of capital's business cycles, sucking people in when the economy soars, evicting them when it dips. Ditto now in the city, capitalism's new factory for valorizing capital, where accumulation's messenger boy is interest-bearing capital circulating through spaces, searching out those titles to future ground rents. The process renders workers superfluous, not only from work but from the totality of living space, displacing from dwelling space as it downsizes the workplace. Can accumulation at one pole and relative superfluity at the other continue together, forever, in the city? Won't we reach a point when a kind of endgame sets in, when the General Law of Capitalist Accumulation generalizes its own illegality?

Here, when the rich have banished the poor from its urban core, won't we have reached a strange apotheosis? Won't we have reached an endgame, like in chess, when the contest is over although we continue to feign the moves? When, after little is left on the urban checkerboard besides a few loose pawns and kings, isn't there nothing left to win nor any real possibility of ever winning? Nothing to exploit, nobody to valorize capital?

The progress of urban accumulation lessens the relative magnitude of the variable part of capital, just as it did in the factory of Marx's day. But, like in industry, it can't lessen it entirely. Capital, as a class, needs its minion service workforce of busboys and valet parkers, of waiters and barmen, of cleaners and security guards, of nannies and cooks, of superintendents and doormen. But a push-pull effect has taken hold, a dialectic of attraction and dispossession, a sucking into the city of a relative surplus population together with a banishment from the center. Poor oldtime stagnant populations, as well as floating and latent reserve armies, now embrace one another out on the periphery somewhere, where rents are lower and life cheaper.

The system produces planetary geography as a commodity, as a pure financial asset, using and abusing people and places as strategies to accumulate capital. The process embroils everybody, no matter where. Cities become vortexes for sucking in everything the planet offers: capital and power, culture and people, dispensable labor-power. It's this process that fuels the urban accumulation machine, that makes it so dynamic as well as so destabilizing. For it's a system that secretes a *residue*, chewing people up when needed, spitting them out when they're not.

Residues are something more than relative surplus populations and probably include a fair number of lumpenproletariat. They're minorities who are far and away a global majority. They're people who feel the periphery inside them, who identify with the periphery, even if sometimes they're located in the core. Residues are workers without regularity, workers without any real stake in the future of work. Residues are refugees

rejected and rebuked, profiled and patrolled no matter where they wander. Residues are displacees whose
land has been grabbed, who have been thrown out of
housing, who must seek living space on the geographic
and economic edge. Residues are disenfranchised and
decommissioned people everywhere who feel isolation
strike them deep within. Residues come from the city as
well as the countryside and congregate in a space that's
often somewhere in between, neither traditional city nor
traditional countryside. We might call this somewhere
in between the global *banlieue*. (Remember, the French
word *banlieue* comes from *lieu*, meaning "place," and
bannir, "to banish"; hence "place of banishment.")

A lot of these residues know that when work is contingent life itself is contingent. And with little security,
there's little to lose, and, moreover, little to gain from
playing by capitalism's rules. So what's the point? There
is no point. Some residues play by different rules, beat a
different drum. Others listen to reactionary demagogues
and swing right, embrace populist ravings. Many others
voice muffled hopes from the left. All somehow know the
capitalist game is rigged, that those in power are liars and
cheats. Still more residues know that a career of hustling
and hawking, of wheeling and dealing, of petty criminality, of opioids and outlawing, become coping mechanisms
from the outside to a life that offers no discernible future
on the inside.

One of the problems Marxists face—and I think
Marx knew it might one day become a big problem—is
that many residues have lost their class address. How
can they regain it, find the right doorbell to ring? How

can workers who have no party, no regular workplace or arena for collective bargaining—who have in fact no real public arena at all—how can they find one another rather than find a reactionary demagogue to cheer? Perhaps the more vital question is how can the twenty-first-century's "dangerous classes" become really dangerous? How can they endanger the capitalist system rather than just endanger themselves?

15.

Most Marxists know that Marx infamously dismisses the lumpenproletariat—that band of "vagabonds, criminals, prostitutes," "the demoralized, the ragged," swindlers and tricksters, ragpickers and pickpockets, tinkers and beggars (all his words). These ruffians, Marx says, "dwelling in the sphere of pauperism," are nothing but "the deadweight of the industrial reserve army," trapped in the Lazarus layers of society and generally not, nor ever likely to be, a progressive political force.

In *Capital*, Marx's lack of faith in the lumpenproletariat only redoubles what he'd said some fifteen years earlier. In *Class Struggles in France, 1848–1850*, he'd written about the rise of Louis Bonaparte's Second Empire, and how a lumpenproletariat had helped crush the June 1848 workers' insurrection in Paris. Without this lumpenproletariat, Marx insists, there wouldn't have been any coup d'état, nor any Louis Bonaparte. The latter's banditry were recruited from the most desperate lumpen elements, bought off (for 1 franc 50 centimes a day) to do the bourgeoisie's dirty work. Thus Louis

Bonaparte shines as "the chief of this lumpenproletariat," Marx jokes, as its reactionary embodiment assuming the mantle of power.

Louis Bonaparte deployed a well-honed tactic that sought the only way out of the crisis: "to play one part of the proletariat against the other." "For this purpose," Marx says, "the Provisional Government formed 24 battalions of Mobile Guards, each a thousand strong, composed of young men, from 15 to 20 years. They belonged for the most part to the lumpenproletariat, which in all big towns forms a mass sharply differentiated from the industrial proletariat, a recruiting ground for thieves and criminals of all kinds, living on the crumbs of society, people without a definite trade, vagabonds, people without hearth or furniture, unapologetically with no fixed address."

Doubtless few smart people these days would deny some of the dubious leanings of the lumpenproletariat. That said, perhaps Marx never recognized the logic of his own analysis? Failing revolution, what's to stop this relative surplus population from relentlessly expanding its ranks? What's to prevent those Lazarus layers from becoming a global norm, outnumbering fully paid-up members of a rank-and-file proletariat?

To dismiss all lumpenproletariat as backward is, accordingly, to dismiss a large segment of the global working class. What's more, if the lumpenproletariat could be once bought off to fight for the bourgeoisie, why can't it be encouraged to shift its allegiances, and come over to fight for the other side? Why should the lumpenproletariat necessarily and always be a reactionary force? It's evident that this mass of humanity, when given the right nudge, has periodically awoken from its slumbers.

Another significant aspect of the lumpenproletariat is that it has no aspirations of being bourgeois. It isn't interested in bourgeois respectability, in its rewards and trappings, in becoming upwardly mobile, ascending into the upper classes. The lumpenproletariat is relatively immune from the bourgeoisie's commercial grasp, its advertising, even its dominate ideology. So, although the lumpenproletariat has sometimes been bought off, it certainly hasn't *bought into* the capitalist system. This, if nothing else, ensures that its potential radicality is always there, waiting in the wings.

The ballast of the deadweight has shifted. The lumpenproletariat has become a decommissioned reserve army of labor that nowadays maybe outweighs the active reserve army of labor. As such, it's a mistake, and this is perhaps Marx's mistake, to see the lumpen-proletariat as a bastard ward of labor. Maybe we need to reconsider the lumpenproletariat and what it *might be capable of*—if ever it came together as a collectivity of desperate and deprived people, of poor working-class people. The threat of its latent potentiality is enough to send a frisson through the progressive senses: a specter haunting the reactionary landscape, the popular masses united, actively rejecting populism!

It's curious how some translations of *Capital*, Volume One, don't actually employ the term *lumpenproletar-iat*. Samuel Moore and Edward Aveling's first English edition, for instance, achieved in 1887, opts instead for "dangerous classes." Lumpenproletariat doesn't appear anywhere in Moore and Aveling's efforts, supervised by Engels.[26] I've always wondered why their translation, which International Publishers reissued in New York in 1967, at Volume One's centenary, differed from Penguin's 1976 edition (and Vintage's 1977), translated by Ben Fowkes.

The latter translation was carried out in conjunction with *New Left Review*, a major theoretical mouthpiece of international Marxism since 1960. At the time, its editorial committee was heavily inflected by Trotskyism, and the most seasoned of Fourth International Trotskyists, Ernest Mandel, wrote a long introduction to the text. Whether Trotsky's stamp, another intellectual who scoffed at the lumpenproletariat, had any subtle bearing on the translation, or, conversely, whether Moore and Aveling's reveal their own secret yearning for a class becoming dangerous, is anybody's guess.

In saying this, we should probably give a nod to Bakunin, Marx's great leftist rival. Bakunin sat on the other side of the fence in the First International, championing its anarchist wing. He waxed lyrical about "the flower of the proletariat," which, he said in "Social Revolution and the State,"

> doesn't mean, as it does to the Marxians, the upper layer, the most civilized and comfortably off in the working world, that layer of semi-bourgeois workers. . . . By the flower of the proletariat I mean, above all, those millions of non-civilized, disinherited, wretched and illiterates . . . that great rabble of the people ordinarily designated by Messrs. Marx and Engels by

the phrase at once picturesque and contemptuous of "lumpenproletariat."

For Bakunin, "that rabble which, being very nearly unpolluted by all bourgeois civilization, carries in its heart, in its aspirations, in all necessities and the miseries of its collective position, all the germs of the Socialism of the future." Bakunin is as glowing about the lumpenproletariat as Marx is as damning. But I'm wondering whether their black or white positioning might be better tempered by a shade of gray, by some critical positioning within each man's camp?

A significant twentieth-century effort to raise the lumpenproletariat out of the mire, and critically affirm it as a "dangerous class," came from beyond the white world: Frantz Fanon, the Marxist physician and psychiatrist from Martinique. His opus, *The Wretched of the Earth* (1961), highlighted the role of a black lumpenproletariat in the anti-colonial struggles that swept across Africa during the 1950s. "It is within this mass of humanity," Fanon wrote, "this people of the shantytowns, at the core of the lumpenproletariat, that the rebellion will find its urban spearhead." The lumpenproletariat, he said, "constitutes one of the most spontaneous and the most radically revolutionary force of a colonized people." "Like a horde of rats, you may kick them and throw stones at them, but despite your efforts they'll go on gnawing at the roots of the tree."

Fanon said revolutionary groups and progressive political parties need to find a space for the lumpenproletariat to maneuver. Any struggle for liberty and justice, he reckoned, ought to give its fullest attention to the lumpenproletariat. Or else oppressors and demagogues won't lose the chance to pit the poor against the poor. "If this available reserve of human effort isn't immediately organized by the forces of rebellion," Fanon warned, "it will find itself fighting as hired soldiers side by side with the colonial troops." Faced with an aggressor, the lumpenproletariat has to grasp its own spirit of spontaneous revolt.

Those wretched of Fanon's earth are, needless to say, still among us. The dialectic of colonizer and colonized, we know, hasn't gone away. Its spots have changed; its nature has changed. It is closer to the core now, an internal urban neo-colony, out on the colonizer's *banlieue*. Colonized peoples are still marginalized peoples. Their freedom of subjectivity continues to be denied. They still lack dignity, suffer daily humiliations (especially police humiliations), endure all the privations and exploitations that Fanon described. Indeed, one of the keywords in *The Wretched of the Earth* persists to this day: lack—"*sans*," in Fanon's French. Everywhere we find people *lacking*: without housing (*sans domicile*), without homeland (*sans patrie*), without land (*sans territoire*), without work (*sans travail*), without official identity cards (*sans papiers*), and ultimately without rights (*sans droits*).

Fanon's death was untimely. He passed away a month after *Les damnés de la terre* first appeared in Paris, dying of leukemia in a clinic near Washington, D.C., age thirty-six. He never saw his great book in print. But its message soon became *the message*, soul food for another sort of anti-colonial battle, one raging in the American inner city. By the mid-1960s, the Black Panthers had reincarnated Fanon as their patron saint in their fight against racist oppression and economic exploitation.

In *Seize the Time*, one of the Panthers' founders, Bobby Seale, recounts calling on another founder, Huey Newton, with a copy of Fanon's book under his arm. "Hey, man, have you read this thing?" he asked Newton. "Huey was laying up in bed, thinking, plotting on the man." No, he said, he hadn't. Soon "the brother got into reading Fanon," Seale said, "and, man, let me tell you, when Huey got hold of Fanon . . . [he'd] explain it in depth." Newton understood what Fanon meant about organizing the lumpenproletariat—"if the organization didn't give a base for organizing the brother who's pimping, the brother who's hustling, the unemployed, the downtrodden, the brother who's robbing banks, who's not politically conscious, that if you didn't relate to these cats, the power structure would organize these cats against you."

Another Panther to get Fanon was Eldridge Cleaver. He was just out of prison, on parole. On the inside, he'd read the *Communist Manifesto* and written letters about his incarceration, about a life of petty crime and the reality of the colonized "black soul." The free-wheeling counter-cultural magazine *Ramparts* published extracts of these letters (which later became the basis for Cleaver's memoir *Soul on Ice*). In Cleaver, Seale saw another Malcolm X. The dude could write, could rap, and he came from the lumpen. Immediately, Cleaver became the Panthers' "Minister of Information." The real work for the Party, he suggested, was "organizing the brothers on the block."

A newspaper was a vital organ. In 1967, *The Black Panther* was launched, beginning as a 4-page newsletter, but quickly becoming a full-blown weekly newspaper, one of the nation's highest circulating underground papers, selling 125,000 copies per week. It relayed information about the party's activities and ideology, as well as other national and international Black struggles. The newspaper connected local needs with larger radical issues, across the United States and the imperialist globe. Ex-cons, without jobs, who'd barely finished high school, who'd never written a line, were working at the newspaper, learning new skills while becoming politically organized and conscious.

In *The Black Panther*, Cleaver published his classic essay, "On the Ideology of the Black Panther Party," pointing the finger at the labor unions, the Democratic Party, and the "Marxist-Leninists." Cleaver reckoned the working class is "the right wing of the proletariat, and the lumpenproletariat is the left wing." "O.K. We're the lumpen," he said. "Right on. The lumpenproletariat are all those who have no secure relationship or vested interest in the means of production and the institutions of capitalist society . . . who have never worked and never will." We're the "criminal element," too, he said, "those who live by their wits, those who don't even want a job, who hate to work and can't relate to punching some pig's time clock, who would rather punch a pig in the mouth and rob him than work for him." But "even though we are lumpen," Cleaver said, "we are still members of the Proletariat, a category that theoretically cuts across national boundaries."

So, "WHO SPEAKS FOR THE LUMPENPROLETARI-
AT?," wondered Cleaver, in a question still requiring a
hard answer. The lumpen finds itself in a peculiar predicament with respect to the *working* working class. It's
been locked out of the economy, sometimes locked itself
out. It doesn't engage in direct action against the system
of oppression; doesn't focus rebellion on the picket line;
can't call a strike against the factory bosses. The lumpen
can't manifest its complaints through any labor union.
"It's forced to create its own forms of rebellion," Cleaver said, "which are consistent with its condition in life."
The lumpen is left with little choice "but to manifest its
rebellion in the University of the Streets."

"Streets belong to the lumpen," Cleaver said, "and it
is in the streets that the lumpen will make their rebellion." This militant reasoning "is often greeted by hoots
and howls from the spokesmen of the working class in
chorus with the mouthpieces of the bourgeoisie. These
talkers like to put down struggles of the lumpen as being
'spontaneous,' 'unorganized,' and 'chaotic and undi-
rected.' But the lumpen moves anyway, refusing to be
straightjacketed or controlled."

Spontaneity always expresses itself in the street. The
street is the last bastion of society that hasn't been entirely dominated by bourgeois institutions (and it's crucial it
stays that way). Institutions fear the street, try to cordon
off streets, repress street spontaneity, reaffirm order in the
name of the law. We know enough from past street revolts
involving lumpenproletariat that streets fill the void left
by institutions. Sometimes mass violence in the street
is unavoidable, even justifiable: it reveals the glaring lag

between "the people" and degenerate social institutions, including out-of-touch politicians.

16.

There's a deep history of ruling classes fearing the dangerous classes and stigmatizing their streets and neighborhoods. The French historian Louis Chevalier long ago showed how dangerous class criminality was often simply a strategy to survive an urban environment where the odds were stacked against poor people. Chevalier's laboratory was Paris, and in *Labouring Classes and Dangerous Classes* (1958) he concentrates on the first half of the nineteenth century, when the criminal activity of the Parisian dangerous classes set a capitalist precedent and became the most normal aspect of urbanizing everyday life.

Chevalier was a historian who'd weaned himself off statistical facts gleaned from official archives. He favored instead the rich descriptions of the great nineteenth-century novelists, particularly Balzac, Chevalier's hero, whose epic *Comédie humaine* (comprising some 91 novels) represented a vast document of social realism, a tremendous historical resource to be tapped. Balzac's novels, Chevalier said, sharply define the link between the dangerous classes and the upper classes, with the "honest" laboring classes wedged somewhere in between.

Balzac remained a lifelong royalist. But he hated an ascendant bourgeoisie with such spleen that he frequently threw in his lot with the lower classes, whom he lived among and wrote about with considerable compassion and sympathy. The backdrop of his creative universe was the collapse of the *ancien régime* (which he lamented) and the massive demographic and economic changes the French capital was undergoing from the 1830s onward. "This unbalanced development of resources and population," Chevalier pointed out, meant "crime was now an aspect of poverty."

Chevalier, like Balzac (and Darwin), uses Malthus's *Essay on the Principle of Population* (1798) as grist. Malthusian ideas were much in vogue then; and the claim that lower-class population growth was rapidly outrunning available resources was heartily cheered by a Gallic gentry across the Channel. Balzac seems to have swallowed Malthusian thought wholesale, without really thinking about it, without really considering its reactionary implications. From the Malthusian standpoint, the rise of the dangerous classes was directly correlated to a depletion of economic resources; there are just too damn many of the buggers, breeding like rabbits, swelling their ranks through an "absolute" law of population the likes of which Marx decried in "The General Law of Capitalist Accumulation." There, he'd said that the creation of wealth *progressively produces a relative surplus population*. Nothing absolute about it.

The Malthusians were dead against social welfare; it would mean the poor would only reproduce even more numerously. The fertility of dangerous classes had to be curbed; beggars should either be sent to the workhouse or kicked out of town. Malthus himself was merciless in denying relief to the poor, instrumental in helping pass the Amendment Act of 1834 Poor Law, revising existing legislation. He said it had been too easy for the poor to receive aid and they were abusing the old system. Kicking them off welfare was in their best interests; it would force the lazy blighters to spend less time fucking about. It was a precursor of classic conservative pretzel logic that prevails to this day.[27]

In Balzac's Paris, proletarians were dangerous because of their desperate situation on the margins of an urban life in transition. Bourgeois capitalism and its factory system was upsizing the city while downsizing the petty-bourgeois artisan, converting the latter into a mere de-skilled wage laborer. And technological change would soon see off the factory hand, chase them onto the streets where what Marx called the "hospital" of pauperism awaited them. Like everything else under capitalism, pauperism is actively "produced." "Its production," says Marx, "is included in that of the relative surplus population, its necessity is implied by their necessity; along with the surplus population, pauperism forms a condition of capitalist production, and of the capitalist development of wealth."

Marx, too, was an admirer of Balzac. Allusions to Balzac's writings are scattered throughout Marx's works. Marx was even reputed to be planning a monograph devoted to the creator of *La Comédie humaine*; alas, he never realized it. Engels was another fan, once remarking in a letter (to the radical journalist Margaret Harkness) that "one of the greatest features in old Balzac" is his "Social Realism."

> His satire is never keener, his irony never bitterer, than when he sets in motion the very men and women with

whom he sympathizes most deeply—the nobles. And the only men of whom he always speaks with undisguised admiration are his bitterest political antagonists, the republican heroes of the Cloître Saint-Méry, the men, who at that time (1830–36) were indeed the representatives of the popular masses.

It's all the more surprising, then, why Marx and Engels should home in exclusively on Balzac's top-down perspective, on his excoriations of "the nobles." Why overlook that other aspect of his social realism: its bottom-up picaresque evocations of the dangerous classes? Marx and Engels make short shrift of Balzac's explorations of their habits and hopes, of their shiftless cacophonous world, which he depicts with both charm and menace. They seem content to have Balzac take apart the elites, without seeing how some of his most fascinating and intriguing characters are poor, hailing from the lowest depths of the popular masses.

Take the criminal genius Jacques Collin (aka Vautrin, aka the Spanish priest Abbé Carlos Herrera). Collin was a master of disguise and dissimulation, Balzac says, a dab hand at ruse and seduction. In his assorted guises, he haunts the whole of Balzac's oeuvre, quite literally haunts it, epitomizing how the shadowy dangerous classes could unnerve the bourgeoisie. Bourgeois society had helped create this species; but its very being, its very underground existence, its dark satanic reputation, became a constant source of terror for ruling classes.

Balzac was quietly protective of Jacques Collin, could never quite bring himself round to kill off his criminal hero. At the end of *Splendeurs et misères des courtisanes*, Balzac has Collin negotiate his own release from Paris's Conciergerie prison, afterward hanging up his swag bag and "retiring in 1845 or thereabouts." Collin's nickname was "Trompe-la-Mort" (Dodgedeath) because of his uncanny knack of escaping incarceration, his hair's-breath avoidance of the gallows. Collin belonged to a highly organized secret criminal association that seemed to mesmerize Balzac: *la haute-pègre*—the high underworld—a diverse network of malefactors in which the lowest of the low seemed to attain the highest of the high. Jacques Collin reigned as its king and mastermind, as its ringleader and royalty.

The high underworld had its own argot and secret language, its own passwords and codes of behavior, its own cells and organizations within organizations, operating in a subterranean hideout of dives and inns, of curtained backrooms and seedy bordellos. Members of the *haute-pègre* considered themselves above the law. In *Splendeurs*, Balzac says "these dukes and peers of the underworld had founded, between 1815 and 1819, the famous society of the '*Dix-Mille*,' so-called from the agreement by virtue of which none of them undertook an operation in which the loot was less than *ten thousand* francs." The *haute-pègre* existed as an underground republic, as a shadow democracy, which, Balzac claims, "presents in the social scene a reflection of those illustrious highwaymen whose courage, character, exploits and eminent qualities will always be admired."[28]

LOUIS CHEVALIER PRODUCED two other works on

the dangerous classes: *Montmartre du plaisir et du crime* (1980), on Paris's famous northern bohemian *quartier* in the first half the twentieth century, with its artists, low-lifes, and *mauvais garçons*; and another, *The Assassination of Paris*, three years earlier, devoted to a different sort of criminal dangerous class, a lumpenbourgeoisie. This time the perpetrators were more dangerous than ever before, principally because they came from the "respectable" high life and wore suits and ties: the *polytechniciens*—the elite bureaucrats educated at France's *grandes écoles*—who'd systematically orchestrated a deadly coup de grâce.

This dangerous dangerous class has instigated a greedy feast—a *grande bouffe*—of rape and urban pillage. Technocrats, in cahoots with a new breed of neoliberal business executives, more brazenly entrepreneurial than their forebears, frequently schooled in the United States, had reorganized Parisian space, done it rationally and profitably in their own crass class image. The wrecker's ball had torn into medieval neighborhoods, emptying them of their popular life, built superhighways along the Seine, ripped out old market halls. "Paris is now a closed universe," Chevalier said, "disinfected, deodorized, devoid of the unexpected, without surprises, with nothing shocking, a well-protected ordered world."

Chevalier saw the destruction of Les Halles, Paris's central wholesale food and flower market, with its wonderful old glass and cast-iron pavilions, as *the* violation of the City of Light, a fatal blow. "With Les Halles gone," he said, "Paris is gone." It had been the heart and soul of Paris, its ignoble viscera, a palpitating living tissue attached to the rest of the city by nerves and ligaments. Such "radical surgery" augurs badly for the popular future of the city, Chevalier thought. The bloody smell of Les Halles—the authentic odor of its working class streets, of butcher's shops and triperies, flower sellers and cheap cafés—had been supplanted by that "frightful jumble of pipes and conduits and ducts that they have dubbed the gas works."

Chevalier meant the Centre Pompidou, "baptized after my unfortunate comrade," he said, "whom I cannot bring myself to believe was personally responsible for this horrible thing." "It is blue," Chevalier quipped, "yet Paris is gray." He'd been a schoolmate of the French president, still lunched with him almost every week; yet Chevalier ventured into a demimonde where his president never ventured and loved the democracy of old Les Halles, where people from all walks of life and classes—from high society to no society at all—once mingled. "In the old popular neighborhood from which all the bums have been removed," he lamented, "one now meets only countless copies of the mink-coated woman walking her dog. Thank God, the dogs at least are not all of the same species. As for the bums, I put among them, without hesitation, those most cherished children of Parisian historians."[29]

Chevalier's attack on planners and urban managers in *The Assassination of Paris* was perhaps the first challenge to the emergence of a new brand of city, underwritten by a new kind of economic philosophy: the neoliberal city, dominated by a dangerous *rentier* class of neoliberals who over the course of the 1980s and 1990s would supersede the *ancien* urban *régime*. The popular city everywhere began wilting under a historic compromise between a neo-managerialist class and an ascendant cadre of free-market businessmen. They would soon join into a hybrid Frankenstein: entrepreneurs transmogrifying into state managers and state managers into commercial entrepreneurs, embracing one another on the threshold of urban change and global capitalist transformation.

At the new millennium, this new order was well and truly over its birth pangs. As it stands to date, the assassination of all big cities has been perpetrated by a shadowy criminal underworld similarly beyond the law. The only difference now is that this underworld makes the law, rules governments, controls mass media and the police, operates unashamedly overground, across the planetary airwaves, peddling its credos and crudities 24/7. This lumpenbourgeoisie also presents itself with an irreconcilable contradiction, an insuperable dialectic of neoliberal economy. On the one hand, its laws of motion suck in and spit out a residual surplus population as a condition of its billionaire wealth production; on the other hand, this order begets the neoliberal city, which wants to rid itself of this selfsame relative surplus population, cleanse its streets of people who have no place to go and who won't disappear.[30]

17.

What can today's dangerous classes learn from yesterday's? When Balzac was scribbling away in the 1830s and Marx still a fresh-faced lad, another kind of clandestine society—"the Society of the Seasons"—met, countenancing conspiracy as one method for instigating insurrection. Its leaders, like the *haute-pègre*, went largely unseen; secret meetings recruited foot soldiers from the intelligentsia and lumpenproletariat, who all pledged allegiance within a hierarchy of cells—a "week" meant six men and a leader; a "month," twenty-eight members plus a leader; three months made a "season," and four seasons a "year." This network hardly stretched beyond Paris; its membership never topped a thousand revolutionaries, around three years of "seasons." Yet the covert nature of its cells unsettled the powers that be, and meant the society punched above its weight—or else seemed to threaten to.[31]

Maybe the Society of the Seasons offers some suggestive hints about what needs to be done now. Maybe we could experiment with a similar seasonal underground today. That way we might avoid those dangerous classes—as Fanon and the Black Panthers had insisted—getting recruited by the enemy, woo them over instead to participate in a new progressive movement, one in which Black and white lives matter. Just as it did almost two centuries earlier, this society would need to establish covert cells in the faubourgs and *banlieues*, setting up leaders and organizers there. Full-time organizers and tacticians could then spearhead a plot to stymie the dominant flow of things.

Against a backdrop of rising unemployment, precarity, and alienation, autonomous leftists of different stripes and persuasions—Black bloc anarchists and dangerous classes who've never been politically active before, men and women, Blacks and whites, gays and straights, trans and cis, *casseurs* and *voyous* (and *voyelles*)—all need to be somehow encouraged to join in, welcomed into cells, so they can positively channel their energies and dissatis- factions. Sites of encounter wouldn't be fancy: ordinary cafés and bars, street corners and youth centers in the peripheral estates, bowling alleys and pool halls at the local mall, school and university cafeterias, independent bookstores, anywhere young people might hang out. Dialogue might sometimes be online but preferably face- to-face. Secrecy would be paramount during plotting, given how the forces of law and order crack down on subversive activity, tainting everything alternative, any- thing it doesn't like, as criminal and/or "terrorist."

One advantage to those without work is, of course, that they have free time. Why not use this precious time socially? Fill it with other people, talking about one's own predicament, which is other people's predicament. Meeting people without jobs or with irregular jobs lets isolated people feel less isolated, creating a conscious collective with time on its hands, discussing publicly political affairs. Many unemployed people are glad they no longer have a life on the rack. But the perpetual men- ace is bureaucratic harassment and humiliation, con- stant institutional intrusion into private life, the burden of proving you're "actively seeking" pointless work that nobody really needs, that nobody would ever miss, that lasts too long and pays too little.

Many people, from the far right to the far left, are always struggling against unemployment, always try- ing to dam its torrential flow. It's never going to work. Many see unemployment as a dirty word, a negative label, a pathology. To be unemployed is to be a person without work. But must we forever define ourselves by work, as workers, and nothing else? Marx taught us why unemployment will never be eradicated from our society, such as it's organized and run. The factory is going badly; so you lay off workers. The factory is going well; so you invest in new technology and lay off workers. It's a no-win situation—for everybody except the bosses and shareholders.

Work for the vast majority of people means time spent doing something that has absolutely no meaning for the doer: an alienated activity, with an alienated product (if there is a product), commandeered by an alienating organization, all conspiring to shape an alienated self. Many twenty- and thirty-somethings these days are learning how to reevaluate their "career" choices, as well as the whole notion of career itself, because they're smart enough to know that they might not have anything deemed "career" anymore. In fact, there's now a whole generation of college-educated twenty-somethings who recognize they'll never work a "proper" salaried job. They're not turned on by temping or interning, either, by any "gig economy." They're a new lumpenproletariat.

Perhaps we can scheme alternative survival programs, other methods through which we don't so much "earn a living" as "live a life." Perhaps we can self-downsize and confront the torment of work that forever jars: work is revered in our culture yet at the same time workers are becoming superfluous. You loathe your job, your boss, loathe the servility required by what you do, by how you do it, the pettiness of the tasks involved, yet want to keep your job at all costs. You see no other way of defining yourself other than through work, than what you do for a living. Perhaps it's time for us to get politicized around non-work. Then the lumpen might really become dangerous.

These are "truths" that any Society of the Seasons might promote and disseminate. In its Marxist guise, organization needs to begin again underground. The underground was the stomping ground for lumpen radicals in the 1960s and it has to be again. But a new underground. Agitate again, build up again, somewhere cheap, somewhere far away. Or perhaps close by. Yet underground. For it's true today that truth is more truthful in the poor underground than in the wealthy overground. Truth won't be voiced from the rich core, but from the poor periphery, from the margins of life, from the margins of our cities, from bedsits and sunken basements, from communal squats, from grungy *banlieues*, from broken-down informal *zones à défendre* (ZAD), defended everywhere.

The other likelihood is that truth will get communicated via old means not new media. It will be shared by word-of-mouth, and on paper, in print form, not just online. Eldridge Cleaver was right to emphasize the importance of a newspaper in organizing, with real pages. We need one, probably more than one, coexisting comradely, not at each other's throats. We need to reinvent the underground press of the 1960s and 1970s, put a fresh spin on this old idea, and inspire a new audience of readers out there now. In their day, newspapers like *Ramparts* so rattled the conservative establishment that the CIA spied on them. (In its pages, *Ramparts* exposed the CIA's surveillance and caused a huge uproar.)

In the late 1960s, there were around 500 underground newspapers, each belonging to the Underground Press Syndicate. All were run as collectives, frequently home-baked, printed on shoestring budgets; editorship usually identified with the counter-culture, with drop-outs and marginals. Some of the best-known papers, like *The Berkeley Barb* and *Rat Subterranean News* (in a wink to Fanon?), had widespread and loyal readerships, shining because of the integrity of their reporting and the quality of the writing. News stories had an honesty that commercial media never had or lost long ago.

The problem with today's commercial media, especially social media, is its saturation: there's just too much of it, too much peddling of lies, too much fear and loathing. Over the airwaves, we're literally flooded with truths, making it hard to decide which truth isn't a lie. Through the underground press other truths might emerge, from the bottom up, like they once did, via the tried and tested printed word, in a newspaper you can trust, that brings integrity to its reportage, correcting mainstream bias and online distortion.

And from the undergrowth a new underground might take hold, together with some new propositions, affirming a different kind of citizenship; not an official citizenship but a sense of identity inside and beyond a passport, inside and beyond any official documentation, any right bestowed by the bourgeois nation-state—underneath it, perhaps, maybe relating more to the city-scale. At this point I can only label it something phantom-like, a *shadow citizenship*, something haunting, lying latent: the repressed will of masses of people yet to find a dangerous collective self.

18.

Marx himself was a kind of shadow citizen moving in the underground, creating a groundswell within capitalism's infrastructure. Like all underground figures, he was marginalized from mainstream society, chose to be so, had a calling to do so. It was a perspective from which he could better express the negative capabilities of a dissatisfied character. Marx's life and thought was a will to flow in his own counterflow. At the same time, he wanted to build structures that could ensure that this counterflow became the new course of society. *Capital* became his "notes from underground," the underground made public, the theoretical subsoil from which new roots could push up and dislodge old established ones.

But Marx's underground is something quite different from the "classic" underground of Marx's contemporary, Fyodor Dostoevsky. Dostoevsky had published his novella *Notes from Underground* three years prior to *Capital*. Dostoevsky's famous "Underground Man" is an isolated individual, withdrawn from society, alone. He isn't a family man with children, like Marx. He's a man who apparently doesn't need other people. He's had enough with utopian thought, too, with its rational paradigms of the Good Life, with its rosy futures where everything is taken care of, sorted for evermore. The Underground Man calls these paradigms "crystal palaces." There, he says, all contradictions would be flattened and there would be no doubt about anything.

Dostoevsky speaks about a long-suffering Underground Man having a "hysterical craving for contrasts and contradictions." He wonders whether human beings like something else besides prosperity. Maybe, he asks, we like suffering just as much? Suffering means doubt, means negation, and "what would be the good of a 'crystal palace' if there could be any doubt about it?" There would be no room for any negative capability. What worries the Underground Man most isn't whether abolishing conflict is possible but whether it is desirable. He hoped people would only love crystal palaces "from a distance," invent them as fantasies, but not want to inhabit them in reality. For living in them means the end of novelty, of adventure and fantasy. Everything would become routine, the death knell of the spirit. Passion would be throttled, and from where, the Underground Man wonders, would intensity of experience, that sole origin of consciousness, then emanate?

I said there are differences between Dostoevsky and Marx; but, in a way, here, they frame things in strikingly similar ways. Like Dostoevsky, Marx's point of departure is that humans are endowed with "vital powers." Vital powers, Marx says, exist in us as "dispositions" and "capacities," as "drives." Marx said this as a young man, in *The Economic and Philosophic Manuscripts*; but it's a position he held even as he grew old, and we can find it in *Capital*. We come to know ourselves by passionately employing these vital powers, he says, feeling, seeing, and comprehending the external world around us, a world that is simultaneously ours and one that incorporates other people.

"To be sensuous," Marx says, "is to *suffer* (to be subjected to the actions of another)." (The emphasis is Marx's own.) Suffering is an "integral human essence," he says, "an enjoyment of the self for man." The Underground Man couldn't agree more! This might sound strange, Marx suggesting that suffering is "an enjoyment of the self." What could he possibly be on about? Surely Marx isn't giving license to the imposition of somebody else's will over the self? After all, isn't that what he was desperately trying to negate?

It's important to remember that Marx was talking *existentially* here. This was his way of affirming the primacy of "free conscious activity" in the "species-character of man," the vitality of free will and individuality. It was why, too, Marx indicts capitalism so ardently; not simply because it makes people suffer—of course it makes people suffer; *Capital* is full of terrible suffering, including the terrible suffering of children.[32] The big problem is that capitalism makes people suffer in a particularly crippling manner. The senses are numbed rather than stimulated; the parameters of free individual development are restricted, despite what capitalists say about freedom.

Marx yearns for a society where people might fully express their individualities and desires, not have them repressed or denied. A big part of people's identities emerges through the act of labor, so important for human well-being and self-worth. Yet wage labor is so utterly senseless, meaningless, and mind-numbing for the bulk of the population. It is suffering without feeling, suffering without thinking, suffering without any value or virtue for the doer. For most people, work actively negates human passion, alienates people from one another. Marx is into what we might call *positive suffering*, suffering without injustice. He wants a society where each human sense—seeing, hearing, smelling, tasting, feeling, thinking, contemplating, sensing, acting, loving (the list is Marx's)—blossoms as "organs of individuality."

Marx's romance of "free development" (there in the *Communist Manifesto* and in the technology chapter of *Capital*) is meant as an alternative to classical and medieval closed societies. It also tells us a lot about what Marx might have thought of Soviet bloc communism had he lived long enough to see it. Marx enjoyed utopian thought, dabbled with it, but in the end rejected it because all its models are crystal palaces. So he and Dostoevsky engage in imagining critical and radical forms of an open society. On that note, they remain existential bedfellows.

Perhaps the biggest contrast surrounds their notion of "underground." For Dostoevsky, the underground is a means of defense, an escape, a site of withdrawal, a place to avoid people, to desist from action and plunge into contemplation. It is diametrically opposed to Marx's conspiratorial underground, where revolutionaries aren't hiding alone under the floorboards, shunning the light of day; they're anonymously laying down channels for practical engagement, for collective action. Marx's underground is a temporary organizing bivouac, not a permanent state of being.

This latter underground probably has more in common with the other famous subterranean realm of modern literature: Kafka's *burrow*. "The Burrow," published in 1931, is a bizarre, unfinished short story, where a mole-like creature burrows an elaborate underworld of tunnels and passageways, with numerous secret escape routes in case of infiltration. The creature's only tool—hence the notion that it is a mole—is "my forehead, that unique instrument." Most of the tale recounts the creature's paranoia about another encroaching creature, which the mole hears, either above ground or burrowing its own tunnel someplace nearby.

"The Burrow" gets under your skin, haunts the reader with its flesh-crawling claustrophobia. It gets to you because the narrative gets inside the head of the beast itself, writes and thinks from its perspective. We hear it musing in its underground: "My constant preoccupation with defense measures," the creature says, "involves a frequent alteration or modification on how the building can best be organized for that end." Extolled is a passion for aloneness and isolation, for defense against a potentially threatening outside reality: "Just think. Your house is protected and self-sufficient. You live in peace, warm, well-nourished, sole master of all your manifold passages and rooms." "Yet," the creature painfully admits, "I am not really free." Indeed, in its isolation and intricate protective tunnels, it has imprisoned itself.

Marx, however, puts another spin on the creature of the mole. A mole actually appears, as a trusty digger, in Marx's underground imagination, yet with much less defensive and individualist overtones than Kafka's. For

Marx, the mole represents none other than the *revolution* itself—the incessant spade work and tunneling that is required to loosen capitalism's foundations, the underground agitation required to make fixed capital crumble underfoot.[33]

We first encounter Marx's "old mole" in Shakespeare's *Hamlet*. It's the ghost of Hamlet's dead father, no longer living but transformed into some strange underground "pioneer":

> *Well said, old mole. Canst work i' th' earth so fast?*
> *A worthy pioneer!*

These are cryptic, somewhat inexplicable lines, yet Marx, the irrepressible reader of Shakespeare, plainly loved the symbolism.[34] Perhaps he knew that even after he was long gone, dead and buried in Highgate Cemetery, the mole would still be digging away at the earth, creating tunnels everywhere in society's infrastructure, pioneering the revolution in his worthy name.

The figure of "old mole" crops up in 1852, in Marx's *Eighteenth Brumaire*. "The revolution," Marx says in section VII of his polemic against Napoleon III, "is thorough-going. It is still in the process of passing through purgatory. It does its work methodically." There's still much collective spade work to be done, Marx says, much digging, much to bring down to earth the ideological superstructure of capitalism. Yet when the foundational groundwork is put in place, Marx declares, paraphrasing his great hero Shakespeare, "Europe will leap from her seat and exultantly exclaim: Well-grubbed, old mole!"

Four years on, Marx's old mole was still at it. In a speech given in 1856, celebrating the anniversary of the Chartists' *People's Paper*, Marx redoubles his furry, well-grubbed imaginary. In the steady work of political agitation and organization, he says, we'll recognize "our brave friend . . . the old mole that can work in the earth so fast, that worthy pioneer—the Revolution."[35]

WHEN I LIVED FULL-TIME IN FRANCE, I remember our old neighbor, Yves, and his wonderful garden. It was his life's project, one he'd resumed in retirement. For years, Yves worked at the post office in Paris's Gare de Lyon. But all he did, when sorting out letters, was dream of our hamlet, a universe away, where he had a house that he and his father had built. Yves was just a lad back then; but years later, as a pensioner, he'd be out every day, at the crack of dawn, no matter what the weather, tending his garden.

It was a French garden, meaning no flowers, nothing fancy; lots of vegetables growing, requiring much weeding. Yves had a lot of land, so he was always mowing the grass, always sorting out his trees with a chainsaw, managing his wood supply for the winter months. He had sheds scattered all around the countryside, where he'd stock his wood, dry it out, years in advance of use, prepared for those rainy days to come. Yet to preserve his rural idyll, to keep it pristine, Yves had to engage in a *civil war*—a civil war against *moles*. Uncontrolled, he said, they'd destroy his lawn, push up the soil into giant molehills, which would wreck the blades of his mower and leave pockmarks all over the grass. It became an obsessive preoccupation for Yves, this war on moles, a bit like Bill Murray's guerrilla war against gophers in the film *Caddyshack*. Yves would set traps and put down all kinds of poison and contraptions that would hopefully see the well-grubbed pioneers off.

He'd sometimes come over to my garden, which was full of molehills, telling me that I had to set traps, otherwise the blighters would see off my lawn completely. I told Yves I couldn't kill any mole; you see, I had a thing about them. One time, when I was young, I had a pet mole. Sort of had a pet mole anyway. I'd found this mole stranded in the middle of the road, on a trip back from Wales with my dad, lost and seemingly dazed by passing cars. I'd taken this mole home for safety, put him in a shoebox filled with bits of torn up newspaper to keep warm, and left sliced white bread for him to eat. By morning, my pet mole was dead, kind of solidified. His little padded pink feet were pointing upward, as if he'd been trying to burrow his way out. We buried him in the garden, returning him to the earth, where he belonged. I never told Yves my mole story; he'd probably think it too sentimental.

Sometime later, we were awoken in the night, in the depths of midwinter, by sounds of cars and a truck stopping outside Yves's house. Actually, it was the *sapeur-pompiers*, the fire brigade, who'd arrived because Yves had had a massive heart attack in bed. They couldn't revive him. But before Yves himself could be buried, strange things began to happen to his beautiful garden. The day after his death, the first molehill appeared. Then, the following day, another. After less than a week, the garden had become a dramatic landscape of mole-hills, pushing up like mini-volcanoes, running rampant from the underground, taking back his land. He had spent half his life embarking on a war of attrition against them. It was a fruitless battle. They won out in the end. You can't keep an old mole down. Not ever.

19.

For much of the 1850s, Marx went underground. Between 1846 and 1852, he'd been one of the main players in the Communist League, a Europe-wide association stretching between Brussels, Paris, Cologne, and London—after Marx had landed there in August 1849. The League's manifesto became the *Communist Manifesto*, drafted by Marx in 1848, addressing "proletarians of all countries." In London, the Communist League was a clandestine group, "a secret propaganda society," Marx had described it, meeting fortnightly in premises along Great Windmill Street, under the cover of a front organization called the German Workers' Educational Association.

It was the beginnings of a party of workers and refugee German intellectuals, conspiring covertly against bourgeois rule.[36] In early 1850, in his address to the Central Committee of the Communist League, Marx said "a provincial interlinking of the workers' clubs is one of the most important points for the strengthening and development of the workers' party." And its "battlecry," Marx said, "must be: 'The Revolution in Permanence.'" But in 1852, the League dissolved, largely at Marx's behest.

There'd been internal doctrinal feuds between London and Cologne branches; some Cologne delegates had also been arrested by the German secret police. There was too much bad blood. Marx said the League's existence was "no longer opportune"; the revolutionary moment, which looked so propitious in the run-up to 1848, had subsided. Better to go underground for a while. Old mole chose to withdraw, and write, tunneling and groundworking in the British Museum.

The 1850s were especially reactionary times, sounding a lot like our own, with a populist backlash against progressive agendas. Marx laid low for most of the decade and began writing and waiting for a future resurgence of the Left. Political fortunes are like economic fortunes: cyclical. In the early 1860s, signs suggested something else was blowing in the wind, another labor upswing was in progress, in France and Germany, and in Poland, where workers had revolted in 1863. Marx feted the Polish insurrection; it filled him with hope that the underground could soon mobilize overground. "This much at least is certain," he wrote Engels, that "the era of revolution has once more fairly opened in Europe." Then, in September 1864, at a mass public rally in London's St. Martin's Hall, working men of different countries assembled to form a "Working Men's International Association." The First International was officially born.

A month on, Marx drafted its charter document, his "Inaugural Address" in a tone that sounded like a dress rehearsal of *Capital*'s "Working Day" chapter. He saluted the Ten Hours' Bill and pushed for a worldwide communist association that "appeared in a form acceptable from the standpoint of the workers' movement." It was a time to take stock, to gather up forces, Marx said, making ready for another organized assault on bourgeois society. We need to think through why the revolutions of 1848 failed, he said, why "all party organizations and journals of the working classes were, on the continent, crushed by the iron hand of force." More optimistically, there had also been, since 1848, a few "compensating features." The Ten Hours' Bill being one, "a great practical success," Marx said, "a victory of a principle; it was the first time that in broad daylight the political economy of the middle classes succumbed to the political economy of the working class."

Nevertheless, there was much still to do, much still to struggle for. One element in the working class's favor, Marx said, is *numbers*. "But numbers weigh," he warned, "only in the balance, only if united by combination and led by knowledge." To disregard the "bond of brotherhood," he said, "which ought to exist between workingmen of different countries, and incite them to stand firmly by each other," would be a recipe for another defeat. "If," Marx wondered, "the emancipation of the working classes requires their fraternal concurrence, how are they to fulfill that great mission with a foreign policy in pursuit of criminal designs, playing upon national prejudices, and squandering in practical wars the people's blood and treasure?"

Marx's political writings of the 1860s deal with the burning question of tactics for building a working class movement. This was the "subjective" element that needed figuring out within the "objective" situation. *Capital* set out this objective political-economic landscape that required navigating. Even when Marx wrote abstract theory, like in *Capital*, he was always thinking about the subjective element, always scheming about concrete practice. Several issues ring out, clearly bothering Marx, and they should still bother us. One was the role of intellectuals like himself: what relationship do thinkers have to workers? The other thing was the underground. How can secret underground organizations become embryos for a larger public movement? This strikes us as something of a conundrum, because if something is expressly clandestine, how can it become widely known, gain greater recognition? How can small secret cells expand and transform themselves into one big powerful organism? Put differently, how does the underground relate to the overground? Or, changing the metaphor: how can moles in the infrastructure also become the "spirits" Marx saw haunting the superstructure?

Marx called for the establishment of "an independent, secret and public organization of the workers' party alongside of the official democrats and make each section the central point and nucleus of workers' societies in which the attitude and interests of the proletariat will be discussed independently of bourgeois influences." This is an awkward and complex sentence, as well as an awkward and complex task to enact. Marx lumps together the secret and public in the same breath, and says nothing about his own role therein. Yet he seems to think that these contradictions are surmountable, that they are answerable through tactical engagement, through some kind of active practice.

The key item resolving the conundrum, that links the secret to the public, the underground to the overground, is a *vanguard*—a vanguard of intellectuals and worker revolutionaries. Marx alludes here and there to such a vanguard, especially in Section II of the *Communist Manifesto*.[37] Yet it was Lenin, half a century later, in his brilliant pamphlet *What Is to Be Done?* (1901), who most vigorously developed the idea, appealing to a vanguard of "*professional* revolutionaries." Now, I've never been very keen on this concept of "professional revolutionaries." It's the nominalized adjective "professional" that jars. Aren't professionals *paid* to do a job, *employed* between certain hours to fulfill a function, on the payroll and thus hired hands? Don't "professionals" have rather narrow specialisms and somewhat blinkered views of reality? The label "professional" gets bandied about all the time these days, as if it guarantees some kind of competence. It doesn't. My experience with professionals is one of incompetence.[38]

Clearly, Lenin didn't see it that way. His point about revolutionaries absorbing themselves wholesale in a mission, devoting their life to a radical political cause, is well taken. Broke Marx was hardly any "professional" revolutionary. But his *vocation* was plainly that of a revolutionary; it was his whole life, his defining identity, his legacy, an act we somehow need to follow. For vocational revolutionaries, making the revolution is core to their being, their life's calling. It isn't a job. Interestingly, Lenin suggests that these revolutionaries are so committed to what they do, have such deep roots, like the well-grubbed old mole, that their belief system "cannot be unearthed."

They're indispensable to the revolution. Better a dozen wise revolutionaries, he says, than a hundred working class fools.

Still, as Lenin frames it, concentrating secret functions in the hands of a small vanguard of professional revolutionaries, "doesn't mean that they 'do the thinking for all' and that the rank and file won't take an active part in the movement." Quite the reverse, he says. "The membership will promote increasing numbers of the professional revolutionaries from its ranks." The role of professional revolutionaries is one of guidance, the wise head that nurtures the collective body. This head is seasoned in the art of political activity, dedicated to the organization, *hardened* to building a revolutionary movement.[39] The vanguard shouldn't incite the visceral passions of the masses, Lenin thinks, as demagogues are wont to do. Demagogues are the "worst enemies" of the working class, he says, since they deliberately stir up emotions that produce misguided conceptions of reality. Who's to argue with that nowadays?

Instead, the movement needs a cool head to strategize, to plan and organize its ranks like a highly disciplined revolutionary army, striking an enemy bourgeois when the moment is right. The vanguard becomes an agitator and organizer, a propagandist and literature distributor. This vanguard sometimes goes underground, but its aim is always to widen the field of its activity, to spread it from one factory to another, from one community to another, from one locality to an entire nation. The most talented agitators, says Lenin, will know how secrecy can ensure the maximum exposure. These agitators may be intellectuals or students; they're probably not likely, for obvious reasons, to be the worker who puts in a ten-hour shift at the plant.

Lenin says a revolutionary vanguard won't unduly affect the participation of the working classes:

> Centralization of the most secret functions in an organization of revolutionaries will not diminish, but rather increase the extent and enhance the quality of the activity of a large number of other organizations that are intended for a broad public and are therefore as loose and as non-secret as possible, such as workers' trade unions, workers' self-education circles and circles for reading illegal literature; and socialist, as well as democratic, circles among *all* other sections of the population. We must have such circles, trade unions and organizations everywhere in *as large a number as possible* and with the widest variety of functions; but it would be absurd and harmful to *confound* them with the organization of *revolutionaries*, to efface the border-line between them. [Lenin's emphases.]

This vanguard of revolutionaries must "go among all classes of the population," go to the people "as propagandists, as agitators, and as organizers," as distributors of newspapers, "which help to establish *actual* contacts with people." Lenin's emphasis suggests that having a newspaper in paper form makes for greater sociability than something which, in our day, might be strictly online. The latter would be a mistake. "This newspaper," he says, evoking some fascinating imagery, "becomes part of an enormous pair of smith's bellows that would fan every spark of the class struggle and popular indignation into a general conflagration." What Lenin describes here is precisely what the *Daily Mail* in Britain does every day in a retrograde direction, fanning a working class scorched earth policy, wiping out its terrain for progressive activity.

It's for this very reason that Lenin thinks class consciousness can be brought to the working class "*only from without*." Socialist consciousness is something introduced into the proletarian struggle from the outside, he says; it doesn't arise naturally and spontaneously inside its ranks. Lenin sees no room for the working class formulating an "independent ideology" by themselves. The only choice, he believes, "is either bourgeois or socialist ideology." There's nothing in between, no middle course. Left to its own devices, left listening to right-wing media, to watching hundreds of channels of commercial TV every night (and day), and reading the tabloid press, the working class is ripe to be duped, fair game to be pump-primed with bourgeois propaganda, having their heads filled with our old bugbear, *false consciousness*.

Marxists need to be constantly on the lookout, ready to contest and demystify the ideological fog that clouds the brains of people, subordinating them to bourgeois ideology. Can we realistically expect a resurgence of a Marxism spearheaded by a revolutionary vanguard, a cohort of thinkers and workers, of activists and unionists still capable of spreading the radical word? Can a small vanguard go to the people like the *Narodniks* of Lenin's generation went to the people?

Maybe this idea of "going to the people" isn't a bad one. In fact, it is probably necessary, what needs to be done for the future of Marxism, for any follower of Marx who wants to be both an underground mole and haunting public spirit. Maybe the task is to go to the people, go as educators and agitators, as critical guides, go to learn about their plight as well as to organize them around that plight. Once, long ago, going to the working class meant going to factories, going to workplaces and communities where you'd find working people en masse. Those factories and collective sites aren't so easy to go to anymore. Many have been downsized and destroyed by deindustrialization, gone under or else there in extremely reduced numbers, hidden and scattered.[40]

These days, to go to the working class is to go to a people without a workplace, without a class address, without a common representative or common sense of belonging. The working class is out there, dispersed everywhere, in zones full of poor and overworked people, among whom 14.3 million and 38.1 million people (in the United Kingdom and United States, respectively) live in poverty. In many ways, these disparate peoples are what Beckett might have called the *unnamables*, a growing mass of the population who've lost their selfhood in a system that has rendered them residual and lumpen, dispensable and manipulable, invisible and divisible.[41]

Contemporary capitalism has downsized and downgraded so many people that there now exists across the globe a huge mass of those *outside* the system. Hence they're a potential cooperative force that could make a great deal of anti-capitalist noise. The paradox is that as its ranks swell, its dwelling space shrinks. With rising property values and rents, people are being priced off the land, "excluded from the very earth as a dwelling place," as Marx said. It's a bit like a Beckett *mise-en-scène*, dramatized by his peculiar specialty: claustrophobic confinement. But in our case it's confinement engendered by a space-hungry, market-driven urban expansion.

As buildings go up, partition walls move in for millions of people. Speculative space opens up, dwelling space closes down, gets sliced up and subdivided, maximizing rents and land values. Wealth for the few resonates as cramped emptiness for the many. In Hong Kong, where accommodation is the most expensive in the world, people now inhabit "coffin cubicles," micro-apartments so tiny that they're not really big enough to fit a cat, let alone swing one. The British living room, too, has shrunk from a 25 square meters average in the 1970s to 17 square meters today for new builds. Britain's lack of affordable housing pushes more and more people into "shoebox" lives.[42] And shoebox lives are a developer's delight. Meanwhile, studies show micro-dwelling negatively affecting health and happiness. And in an increasingly abrasive outside world, cramped life leaves no room for decompression on the inside.

Perhaps Beckett's short story "The Lost Ones" gives us an unsettling sense of those walls closing in, with "one body per square meter or two hundred bodies in all round numbers. . . . The gloom and press make recognition difficult." Is this a vision of the death camps, or refugees in a transit camp? Or is it just a vision of ordinary everyday madness, of multi-occupancy in an unaffordable city, where rents have skyrocketed? Public space on the outside seems equally desolate, more and more resembling the set of *Waiting for Godot*—a main street, with boarded-up stores, a tree, a few vagrants hanging around. We can almost hear Estragon grumbling: "We've no rights any more." "We got rid of them," sidekick Vladimir rejoins.

Beckett's darkest evocation of bare life is *Endgame* (*Fin de Partie*), from 1957. "I once knew a madman," Hamm muses in *Endgame*, "who thought the end of the world had come. I had a great fondness for him. I used to go and see him, in the asylum. I'd take him by the hand and drag him to the window. Look! There! All that rising corn! And there! Look! The sails of the herring fleet! All that loveliness! He'd snatch away his hand and go back into his corner. Appalled. All he had seen was ashes."

At one point, Hamm declares—"*with fervour*"—in Beckett's italics: "I love the old questions. Ah the old questions, the old answers, there's nothing like them!" Somehow this declaration now seems vital, profound and instructive, more than just a few throwaway lines. But what does it mean, what could it mean? Maybe there are some old questions in the Marxist tradition, time immemorial questions, and regardless of the particular forms they take, there is, as Hamm says, *nothing like them*. One old question might be Lenin's *What Is to Be Done?* It has usually provoked an old response: *class struggle, dictatorship of the proletariat*, the founding and organization of a party, a party of and for this proletariat, including its lumpen variant. Perhaps there still isn't anything like it, for letting us see beyond those ashes.

The old party was there to *represent* the interests of the working class, even if some members of this working class weren't interested in joining this party. Nevertheless, the party had the interests of a public in mind. There were services this public needed, public services—social housing, decent education, adequate healthcare, reliable buses, trains, and subways. This public also needed a certain loveliness. Under the old questions, the city itself was never a market: it was a public good, a rich collective works, managed in the public interest, not in the interest of the rich—*not managed by the rich in the interests of the rich*. There was a city government, and this city government had a plan. City governors and city planners were elected officials, constituted by the party in office, who were accountable to "the people," often made up of "the people," with checks and balances that assured democracy was agreed upon.

To be sure, the checks and balances would control what the rich did, how it speculated on those vital public goods, that it couldn't speculate on those vital public goods, that city government needed to ensure its poorest citizens could live in safe and stable neighborhoods. Any Hobbesian war of all against all had to stop, that the overarching public interest had to be maintained. Perhaps the old questions and the old responses can become new solutions again, ending this endgame of ours.

Beckett's focus on poverty and loss, on *lessness*, is maybe the spirit the Marxist tradition needs to resuscitate. A new old Marxism based on immiseration. Perhaps Marxism and Marxists need to take to the streets to see things close up, in the raw, like the vagabond Jean-Paul

Clébert.[43] Perhaps it needs a new epiphany about what it once was. Its theory has lost sight of its subject, abandoned its subject: this residue of neoliberal capitalism, this rank and file, Marxism's real constituency, the Beckettians evicted and exhausted, thrown out of their dwelling space as well as their workspace. It's a global working class whose ranks grow by day yet no longer has its party—indeed has witnessed a *fin du parti*. Is the Labour Party up for being its representative in Britain? The Democratic Party in the United States? I have grave doubts.

Maybe an old question might not be so much Lenin's *What Is to Be Done?* as tweaking his other question: *Where to Begin Again?* After the defeat of the 1871 Paris Commune, Arthur Rimbaud, a seventeen-year-old poet-protagonist, said the blood of its victims drained away all hope for his generation. For a long time to come, Rimbaud said, truth will have to go underground, because it had been reduced to tatters, along with life. Ours is a similar age. To trace out any hope of its recovery, Marxists need to organize underground, follow Old Mole of old, assemble in bedsits, in sunken basements, maybe in communal squats, somewhere cheap, somewhere far away. Or nearby.

There are closing moments in *Capital* when Marx seems to posit that capitalism will implode because of its own internal contradictions alone, without any force built up against it, any subjective element to overthrow it. Near the end of Volume One, we think it's the end, that capitalism's own "immanent laws" are about to destroy it. Here he is, in chapter 32, on "The Historical Tendency of Capitalist Accumulation," letting rip:

Along with the constant decrease in the number of capitalist magnates, who usurp and monopolize all the advantages of this process, the mass of misery, oppression, slavery, degradation and exploitation grows; but with this there also grows the revolt of the working class, a class constantly increasing in numbers, and trained, united and organized by the very mechanism of the capitalist process of production. The monopoly of capital becomes a fetter upon the mode of production which has flourished alongside and under it. The centralization of the means of production and the socialization of labour reach a point at which they become incompatible with their capitalist integument. The integument is burst asunder. The knell of capitalist private property sounds. The expropriators are expropriated.

This seems as good a place as any to stop, to finish *Capital* on an upbeat note, gleefully celebrating the collapse of bourgeois society, its own melting into air. But no, this isn't how Marx's brain operates. Suddenly, he moves against himself, against his own wishful thinking, forcing open his Pandora's box, opening it up to fresh rounds of "primitive accumulation." Pow, now there seems no stopping capital's expansion machine again, spinning off into a colonial orbit (chapter 33). Now the world is seemingly its oyster. New fertile soils emerge to dispossess and privatize, to kickstart the accumulation process anew—in the United States and Canada, in Australia.

Marx had earlier toyed with the "secret" of primitive

accumulation; now he makes it public knowledge. Primitive accumulation, he says, plays the same role for capital as "original sin" does for theologians. It's the starting point of something revelatory, an initiation into virgin territories, into pre-capitalist lands, into "New Worlds," putting in place new social relations of domination. The possibilities for primitive accumulation appear infinite.

Nowadays, primitive accumulation mobilizes high-tech sophistication, plunders modern territories, dispossesses lands and states, invades the whole public realm (privatizing spaces, schools, services, hospitals, infrastructure)—smashing and pilfering where it can, any way it can. Marx ends *Capital* devilishly open-ended because he knows how capital itself is devilishly open-ended. It turns on new axes, gyrates to all manner of new gyrations. What else could the man do but gyrate himself? And what else is there for us to do but gyrate ourselves?

20.

It's late November now, nine months since I began this book, nine months since I last stood in Highgate Cemetery, beside Marx's vandalized grave. It's a chilly autumnal morning, damp and gray, and even before midday the light is already starting to fade. I am here to speak with Ian Dungavell, of The Friends of Highgate Cemetery Trust, who said via email that he'd be more than happy to talk to me about Marx's ransacked resting place and what's been happening there since last February's attack.

Ian is a tall, athletic-looking man in his early fifties. He greets me warmly at the East Wing's entrance, dressed in a black windbreaker bearing the cemetery's logo. As we stroll over to Marx, he talks enthusiastically about his 53,000-grave, 37-acre fiefdom, and what it means to keep it all together, looking after the long as well as recent dead. It's a nonstop task for the Friends, he says; trees forever fall over; weeds and weather erosion overwhelm a lot of old, untended graves. And since people are always dying, there are space constraints. All of this is inevitably costly and time consuming.

The Friends of Highgate Cemetery Trust is a registered charity and survives off donations and gifts from wealthy benefactors. The bulk of the workforce manning the wheelbarrows and entrance points are volunteers, both local Highgate residents, who see the cemetery as part of the neighborhood's heritage, and other Londoners attracted by the specialness of the place. Ian tells me that since they began charging an entry fee in the early nineties (currently £4), finances have perked up, drawing a not-inconsiderable sum when one considers that around 100,000 visitors pass through the cemetery's gates each year. Marx, he says, grabs the majority of grave-spotters' attention. People come from all over the globe to walk around the cemetery, either by themselves, unaccompanied, or in guided group tours. Marx is usually high up on the list of must-sees.

After a couple minutes, we approach Marx and for an instant I hold my breath, wondering what state the great man might be in. *Good news*: the red paint has gone; the marble plinth looks clean and back to normal, just as I remember it from former times. What a relief! "Yes," Ian says, "the attacker used water-based paint, which could be removed with blasts of heated water from a powerful thermal spray. It took the best part of a day for a skilled conservator to get rid of it, but there are still traces of red if you look hard." The attack had probably been carried out in the early hours, Ian recalls, "as when I arrived first thing in the morning, after being notified of what had happened, the paint was still wet."

Marx's grave is quite peculiar at the cemetery because it's actually the domain of the Marx Grave Trust, a different charitable organization. The Grave Trust owns and maintains Laurence Bradshaw's Marx tomb, inaugurated in 1956, at a ceremony presided over by Harry Pollitt, then the British Communist Party's General Secretary. Bradshaw, an artist and sculptor, was himself a Party member, had been since the early 1930s. His most famous work was designed "to be a monument not only of a man," Bradshaw said, "but to a great mind and great philosopher." He wanted the site to convey "the dynamic force of Marx's intellect." Which is probably why he made it so big. Since 1974, the bust and headstone have been designated a listed monument, reaching the highest Grade-1 status in 1999.

Thus the bust and headstone are the Marx Grave Trust's responsibility, not ours, Ian says. Though, obviously, "we've been working together to supervise the repairs." The marble tablet looks like it's on the mend, too, after it had been brutally and maniacally walloped with a lump hammer. I run my hands over it, touch the lettering with my palm, only to discover that it's a mock panel. It's really a photo printed on the plastic board that realtors use to advertise their wares; the giveaway is that if you look closely you can see the screws holding it in place. "Ah," Ian says, "that's our little trick for the time being." "The Grave Trust is still trying to decide what to do with the original tablet. One suggestion is to replace it behind reinforced glass, but," he says, "I'm not so keen on that."

To prevent further attacks, "some want to put the whole tomb behind high railings." Again, says Ian, he's against it. People can always climb over. "What are we to do? Put up barbed wire around it? It's a cemetery, and that sort of thing seems out of place, even distasteful, here. To convert the place into a prison seems wrong to me," he maintains.[44] "I think what shocked people most about last February's vandalism was its ferocity, that it was a terrible violation. Whatever your views about Marx, cemeteries are sites of peace, reflection and remembrance, not places of aggression and violence." After a brief pause he continues, "It's really interesting, isn't it, how certain people would want to go to such lengths to smash Marx. What is it about the man and his ideas that seem to threaten people so much after all these years? Do they really think they're going to destroy the ideas by destroying the grave? It's interesting how people feel so afraid of Marx. Is there any other intellectual throughout history that is like that?"

We lighten the conversation for a minute, joke about the flowers left around the base of the plinth. The Sainsbury's supermarket tag is still vividly apparent on some of them, bearing the price £2.98, "reduced from £4." "You'd have thought they'd have at least taken the price

tag off," Ian says. We laugh together. And we agree: surely Marx is worth more than even the original £4!

Ian has a PhD in architectural history and is keen to
point out some of the fine-grain features of Bradshaw's
original design. Marx's plinth is Cornish granite, but it
is only a covering, he says. Inside is brick. "It would have
been better if the entire structure were solid granite. Yet
in the mid-1950s it was clearly too costly for the British
Communist Party who paid for it." If you look closely you
can see traces of previous attacks, like the National Front
bomb from the 1970s. One time, in the 1960s, Ian says
somebody tied a rope around Marx's massive bronze bust
and toppled it. The bronze head was found on the ground.
It was put back, he says, "and is now firmly attached to
the plinth, thank goodness!" The 1960s, apparently, was
a dismal period for the cemetery, when it fell on finan-
cially hard times. The owner then was a pretty horrible
property developer, Ian tells me, who wanted to sell Marx
to the Soviets, and ship his whole tomb and remains to
Moscow. But the Russians, with their own problems dealing with embalmed Lenin, weren't interested.

The two-meter-square patch immediately in front of
the grave is now paved over with black granite. "That
was paid for by the Chinese government," Ian says. "We
wrote to them asking for a contribution and they obliged
by financing the whole amount." In fact, he confirms
that the Chinese are among the most frequent visitors
to Marx's grave. Just yesterday, Ian says, "around 3:50
pm, ten minutes before the cemetery was due to close,
a minibus rolls up full of wealthy Chinese businessmen,
dressed immaculately in suits, wanting to see Marx. This

happens quite often, Chinese businessmen coming to see Marx. On these occasions, I feel a responsibility for showing them around personally, even if it is after hours. Marx continues to fascinate the Chinese."

It's ironic, I think to myself, how for decades the Chinese people were force-fed Marx when their peasant society could hardly digest him. Marx's thought, outlining the inner contradictions and human misery stemming from modern industrial capitalism, was poorly suited to agrarian China. Only now, with China's massive and dramatic industrial development, do they seem ready to really get Marx. Doubtless, these businessmen know it. With the Chinese state combining the worst features of capitalism and communism, now its citizens can begin to see how Marx might be their future guide. He's somebody who can lead them into their modern-day, twenty-first-century industrial contradictions, together with the class antagonisms that'll likely reveal themselves in the years ahead. China's engagement with Marx—dead and alive—may only just be beginning.

Standing in front of Marx with Ian Dungavell, I remember *High Hopes*, Mike Leigh's 1988 tragicomedy, the British director's take on the fear and misery of Thatcher's third term. It had been a long time since he had seen it, Ian says. In one memorable scene, Leigh's hero Cyril and heroine Shirley jump on their motorbike to pay homage to old Marx here at Highgate. The duo is all out of sync with the value system of their age, with the Iron Lady's greedy individualism. They're happily shacked up in a condemned little council flat behind King's Cross, two socialists a bit lost in the free market world, wondering what's left, what's to be done to survive. Cynicism and despair almost overwhelm Cyril; but Leigh's humor, and Shirley's love, keep him fresh, keep his hopes high. So off they go, up to Highgate Cemetery, Cyril and Shirley, on a Marx pilgrimage; and like Ian Dungavell and me today, they stand before Marx, confronted by that huge bust and colossal brain.

"He's a bit big, in'ee?" says Shirley. "He was a giant," says Cyril. "No, I mean 'is head," Shirley qualifies. "He's all right," says Cyril. "What he done was he wrote down the truth. People was being exploited. The Industrial Revolution—they was forced off the land into the factories. There weren't no working class before then. Marx set down a program for change." "I wish I'd brought some flowers now," says Shirley. "Don't matter, does it, flowers," Cyril quips. "What d'ya mean, it don't matter?" Shirley asks, surprised. "He's dead," Cyril says. "Well, you're goin' on about 'im," says Shirley. "I'm talking about his *ideas*," Cyril says. "I know," says Shirley. Then she reads the inscription on the plinth: *Philosophers have only interpreted the world in various ways; the point, however, is to change it*. "There you are."

Shirley wanders off, inspects the other graves and the cemetery's wild flowers. Cyril stays put, ponders over Marx's quote. He says nothing, just gazes up at the bust. He's so close to Marx that he's almost looking *under* the revolutionary's massive chin, eyeing his bearded profile from below, his forehead and protruding brow, his huge bushy eyebrows around those intense eyes staring out. Cyril stares, too, but in wonderment, in some strange personal cosmic reverie. Mike Leigh gives us a long, quiet frame, a sequence not risked very often in modern action-obsessed commercial cinema. The camera lingers on Marx. Nothing happens. All we hear is the gentle breeze, the birds, and Cyril's inner thoughts, his doubts, his admiration.

We listen to Cyril's brain ticking. Marx's inanimate bronze seems to be listening too, cogitating with Cyril, alive among the cemetery's dead. Suddenly, Cyril jolts out of his reverie, and blurts aloud: "The thing is, change what? It's a different world now, innit? By the year 2000, there'll be 36 TV stations, 24 hours a day, telling you what to think." Then another pause, another quiet reflection; then, out of the blue, almost arguing with himself: "Pissing in the wind, innit." It's the "innit" that suggests Cyril isn't quite sure, that maybe following Marx mightn't really be pissing in the wind, and that even pissing in the wind is to relieve oneself.

Parting with Ian Dungavell, I thank him, we shake hands, and he's gone, off up the lane back to work, leaving me alone with Marx and my camera. I took a photo (see page 173), from Cyril's perspective. Then I think: Marx knew how capitalist society was a sorcerer that mesmerizes people, that has us piss in the wind, believe in the crap it feeds us. In the *Manifesto*, he said, "Modern bourgeois society" had even mesmerized itself, that its ruling class "is no longer able to control the powers of the nether world they've summoned up with their spells." This is especially worrying now, because never has modern bourgeois society been so full of conjuring tricks as today, carried out by joker politicians who have lost all control of what they're doing, of what they ought to be doing; they long ago lost contact with ordinary people's everyday reality. But that doesn't seem to bother them, nor bother the people they govern. They have cast spells the likes of which we've never seen before. They have become sorcerers of collusions and conspiracies, of tricks and deceptions, of fake news and endless, unbelievable sleights of the economic and political hand. Bizarrely, many people seem to *want* to believe these sleights of hand, this smoke and mirrors, this visceral wand-waving that summons up the emotions, the *unthinking* senses. The greatest spell they've cast is that we can't see how they've turned us into toads.

IT'S TIME FOR ME TO LEAVE MARX NOW, leave the dead Marx at the cemetery. I walk up the lane that Ian took a few minutes earlier, carrying Marx inside me, his living spirit, those ideas that threaten reactionaries so much. Perhaps this spirit can be the kind of counter-magic we need more than ever, something that can transform us back into thinking human beings again. Maybe Marx can give us the critical faculties we need nowadays, to get an analytical grip on the current impasse. I stroll back to the entrance gate. My mind wanders. Our life is afflicted with the insomnia plague that Gabriel García Márquez outlines in *One Hundred Years of Solitude*. When the insomnia plague hits Macondo, the sick person no longer sleeps a wink. At first, the townsfolk aren't alarmed. On the contrary, they're happy in their hallucinogenic state: there's much work to do building up the new town and barely enough time to do it; so much the better, then, if they don't sleep.

But soon people traipse around busying themselves with all manner of inane activities, fidgeting about and telling each other the same old jokes over and over. After a while, the most fearsome aspect of the insomnia plague strikes: memory loss. People forget the past and begin to lack any awareness of the present, of their own being, until they sink into "a kind of idiocy," Márquez says. Meantime, the person no longer dreams, loses the capacity to imagine a future. They enter instead into an eternal present, a senseless state that sounds a lot like our condition today. So-called "screen-time insomnia" does an effective job of numbing us even more. Excessive screen-time, especially from smartphones in bed, affects our brain cells, creating attention span deficiencies and prompting sleeplessness. It's particularly apparent among teenagers. Yet adults seem equally mesmerized by the blue light, muddling our brains as to whether it is actually day or night time. We, too, thereafter, sink into a kind of collective idiocy that makes us easily manipulable.

And yet, in *One Hundred Years of Solitude*, Márquez's hero, the radical liberal freedom fighter, Colonel Aureliano Buendía, conceives a novel method to protect himself against memory loss. As soon as he begins having trouble remembering objects' names, he decides to mark each one with labels. All he has to do is read the inscription in order to identify them. With an ink brush he marks everything with its name. Then he realizes that one day people might also forget not only the names of things, but where they came from, and what use they have. Thus he sticks signs on things, like on a cow, saying: "*This is a cow. She must be milked every morning so that she will produce milk, and milk must be boiled in order to be mixed with coffee to make coffee and milk.*" So it went, to prevent reality slipping away. But the system demanded so much vigilance and moral strength that many succumbed to the spell of an absurd reality.

As our reality seems to slip evermore into absurdity, Marx can help us put labels back on things, help us not forget the value of written letters. He can ensure we remember where things come from, who made them, and how they function in society. The Marxist label recalls that a thing is really a social relation, a social process that requires deeper and wider understanding. Things get enveloped in mist, and we need a thought procedure that can help us grope our way through the haze. Marx's ideas can keep our brains and our bodies alert. They can put our individual lives not only in a relative, collective perspective, but also in some sort of historical continuum. Who we are hinges on who we once were and who we might become in the future. Past and future are internalized in the present, and the present is always open-ended and fluid, never fixed or forever given, written in stone. Nor even cast solid in bronze.

That's the dead Marx. The living Marx can help us stay *vigilant*. He can ward off magic spells, repel the incantations of demagogic magicians. Marx's thought can act as a revelatory power, alerting us to anything phony and false, to hollow promises and lurid conspiracies. For the Marx who is alive, as Cyril says, "It don't matter, does it, about flowers." "Well, you're goin' on about 'im," says Shirley, and it's true, I have been going on about him in this book. "I'm talking about his *ideas*," Cyril says, helping me along. "I know," says Shirley. I can hear Shirley in my head now, reading the inscription on the grave's plinth: *Philosophers have only interpreted the world in various ways; the point, however, is to change it.* "There you are," she says afterward. There you are indeed.

Notes

1.   "One day," Shawn's dramatic monologue goes, "there was an anonymous present sitting on my doorstep—*Volume One of Capital* by Karl Marx, in a brown paper bag. Did someone leave it as a joke? Did someone seriously think I should read it? And who had left it there? I never found out. Late that night, naked in bed, I leafed through it. At first it seemed impossible, a sort of impenetrable tangle of obsessively repeated groups of words curling around each other like moles underground, but when I came to the part about the lives of the workers—the coal-miners, the child labourers—I could feel myself suddenly breathing more slowly."

2.   Cited in "After Marx Vandalism, Highgate Cemetery Weighs Security Cost," *The Guardian*, February 24, 2019

3.   Terry Eagleton, *Why Marx Was Right* (New Haven: Yale University Press, 2011).

4.   Peter Stallybrass, "Marx's Coat," in Patricia Spyer, ed., *Border Fetishisms: Material Objects In Unstable Spaces* (London: Routledge, 1997)

5.   Horner did write a memoir in two volumes, published privately and posthumously, in 1890. In 1969, the historian Bernice Martin wrote a portrait of Horner in the *International Review of Social History* 14/3, using this memoir. My own brief sketch of Horner here draws upon Martin's article, downloadable at: https://www.cambridge.org/core/services/aop-cambridge-core/content/view/S0020859000003667.

6.   In early 1860, Marx wrote Engels, telling his friend that "Horner has resigned from his post." "His last short report is full of bitter irony," Marx says. "Can't you find out," Marx asks Engels, "if the Manchester mill-owners had a hand in this resignation?" (Letter, January 11, 1860, in *Marx-Engels Selected Correspondence*, Moscow: Progress Publishers, 1955, p. 121).

7.   Other factory inspectors were equally incredulous of Senior's "fatal hour." In one report, dated May 21, 1855, Marx cites Inspector Howell talking: "Had Senior's ingenious calcula-

tion been correct, every cotton factory in the United Kingdom would have been working at a loss since the year 1850." Evidently, they weren't; business was in fact booming.

8. See "Death from Overwork," *The Guardian*, October 18, 2016.

9. See "Japanese Woman 'Dies from Overwork'," *The Guardian*, October 5, 2017.

10. See "The U.S. Is the Most Overworked Country in the Developed World," *Forbes Magazine*, March 1, 2018.

11. See "Congratulations! You've Been Fired," *New York Times*, April 9, 2016.

12. Ibid.

13. See "School Children in China Work Overnight to Produce Amazon Alexa Device," *The Guardian*, August 8, 2019.

14. It's scary that such drivel actually made it into a "scholarly" text. Ure's *The Philosophy of Manufacturers* was published in 1835, to considerable acclaim.

15. Until quite recently a lot of museum staff were Carillion employees. In early 2018, after the giant management and construction services company went belly-up, with £7 billion in liabilities, some of the staff were brought in-house again. But only because of loud public outcry and a series of worker protests outside the museum. The dispute brought to light the deeper concern of the privatization of Britain's cultural institutions and the misguided decision made by the British Museum's trustees—the "they" in question, presumably. Since 2013, Carillion had negotiated a controversial deal at the museum, where it'd been instrumental in offering zero-hours contracts and slashing staff benefits.

16. It's interesting to consider this with respect to the current American working class, which is made up of far fewer factory workers. To be sure, the real face of the U.S. working class isn't blue collar at all, but the lowly paid woman care-worker who's probably looking after an ex-factory worker. Half of the ten fastest-growing jobs in America are now low-paid variants of nursing. (See "Reviving the American Working Class?," *New York*

Times Editorial, August 29, 2019.) The other thing, of course, is that new manufacturing activity doesn't usually mean more jobs. On the contrary, it invariably means more capital-intensive technology, more robots and computer-aided manufacturing, likely done far away from the shores of America. Dongguan, for example, a Chinese city near Hong Kong, the manufacturing capital of the world, recently launched its first fully automated factory; the shape of things to come.

17. Though some do. In many business-friendly nations, like the United States, corporations finagle compensation for depreciation through generous tax write-offs.

18. In a series of remarkable black-and-white photographs from the West Midlands, John Myers documented the last days of some of Britain's industrial landscape during the early-1980s. The book's title says it all: *The End of Industry*. After the arrival of Margaret Thatcher in 1979, Myers says, "companies folded and factories were demolished at an unbelievably rapid rate in the couple of years after these pictures." The region's industrial heritage was "clobbered overnight." Unlike the northeast's shipyards and the northwest's textile mills, these industries were smaller-scale affairs, chain-making operations, foundries and brickwork firms. Their fixed capital couldn't be rehabbed into upscale warehouse apartments and so most were simply razed, brutally blasted into air, amorally depreciated.

19. Luddites had their allies, among them the great Romantic poet Lord Byron (admired by Marx), whose famous maiden speech in the House of Lords, on February 27, 1812, passionately opposed the bill to make Luddite frame-breaking a capital felony. "Down with all Kings," Byron's sly song went, "but King Ludd!"

20. Gabriella Coleman, *Hacker, Hoaxer, Whistleblower, Spy: The Many Faces of Anonymous* (London: Verso Books, 2014).

21. For the best discussion of Russian evolutionary thought, see Daniel Todes's now-classic essay, "Darwin's Malthusian Metaphor and Russian Evolutionary Thought, 1859–1917," *His-*

tory of Science Society (December 1987): 537–51. For a quirk-
ier take on Kropotkin and Darwin, see the late Stephen Jay
Gould's, "Kropotkin Was No Crackpot," available online at the
Marxist Internet Archive, https://www.marxists.org/subject/
science/essays/kropotkin.htm. When Kropotkin lived in England, the bourgeois scientific establishment was wary of his
evolutionary theories and political anarchism. He once spoke,
on invitation, at the British Association for the Advancement
of Science, and Cambridge University even offered Kropotkin
a chair in geology, provided he quit his political activities. But
Kropotkin turned the university down because he was never
going to quit his anarchist beliefs. In reality, Kropotkin bore
no resemblance to a stereotypical black-masked anarchist. He
was a gentle pacifist, and with his great grandfatherly beard
looked more like an aged monk than any terrorist. He was how
we could imagine Dostoevsky's Alyosha Karamazov appearing as an old man.

22. Walmart's low-wage workers are so poor that they receive
around $6.2 billion in federal assistance, principally in the
shape of food stamps. The billionaire Walton business thus
gets a huge public handout for its low-balling employment
practices. In a recent study, conducted by the Organization
United for Respect (OUR), 55 percent of Walmart part-timers
admitted they didn't have enough money to meet basic needs.

23. See "Google's Shadow Workforce: Temps Who Out Number
Full-Time Employees," *New York Times*, May 28, 2019.

24. See Kriston Capps, "The Hidden Horror of Hudson Yards Is
How It Was Financed," *CityLab*, April 12, 2019, https://www.
citylab.com/equity/2019/04/hudson-yards-financing-eb5-in-
vestor-visa-program-immigration/586897/.

25. See *Marx's Economic Manuscript of 1864–1865* (Chicago:
Haymarket Books, 2017).

26. Neither translator was a professional linguist. Moore was a
socialist judge, based in Manchester, whom Engels knew and
who had earlier translated the *Communist Manifesto*; Aveling
was the common-law husband of Marx's youngest daughter,

Eleanor. For the record, the *Communist Manifesto* does mention the "dangerous classes," "the social scum, that passively rotting mass thrown off by the lowest layers of old society." But, as Marx sees them, the only danger they pose is to themselves.

27. "Let us note incidentally," Marx ironizes in a footnote to *Capital*, chapter 25, "that although Malthus was a parson of the Church of England he had taken the monastic vow of celibacy. . . . This circumstance favourably distinguishes him from other Protestant parsons, who have flung off the Catholic requirement of the celibacy of the priesthood, and taken 'Be fruitful and multiply' as their special Biblical mission to such an extent that they generally contribute to the increase of the population to a really unbecoming extent, whilst at the same time preaching the 'principle of population' to the workers."

28. The *haute-pègre* really existed in the first half of the nineteenth century; and Balzac's Jacques Collin was loosely based on a real-life character, Eugène-François Vidocq. Vidocq was a criminal mastermind who knew so much about this underworld that, in the end, like Jacques Collin, he turned crime against itself, morphing into the first-known private detective and founder of a national detective agency known as the *Sûreté Nationale*. For some time Vidocq assumed a life as double agent, a dialectical spy, though often which way the arrows pointed was blurry. His life of crime and as a criminalist captured the literary imagination of several writers, not just Balzac but Victor Hugo and Edgar Allan Poe (see "The Murders in the Rue Morgue").

29. Guy Debord, who once associated himself with the Parisian dangerous classes in the fifties and sixties, found a strange affinity with the conservative Chevalier. In *Panegyric*, he wrote: "It was almost as though . . . I was the only person to have loved Paris, because, to begin with, I saw no one else respond to this matter in the repugnant seventies. But afterward I learned that Louis Chevalier, the city's old historian, had published then, without too much being said about it, *The Assassination of*

Paris. So we could count at least two righteous men in that city at the time."

30. In UK cities, there's been talk about scrapping a 195-year-old Vagrancy Act (1824). Now, there are so many homeless people sleeping rough and begging on British streets that to criminalize them is both a savage flouting of human rights and an overstretching of police resources. According to the homeless charity Crisis, rough sleeping increased 70 percent between 2014 and 2018; homeless encampments have tripled during the past five years. As Crisis says, nobody should be criminalized for having nowhere to live. See "Calls for 195-year-old Vagrancy Act to Be Scrapped," *The Guardian*, June 19, 2019.

31. The Society of the Seasons was founded by two great republican revolutionaries, Louis-Auguste Blanqui and Armand Barbès, prominent organizers in the armed insurrection of May 1839 and June Days of 1848. Each devoted his life's work to not working, and to conspiring to overthrow the ruling regime. Marx called Blanqui "the head and heart of the proletarian party in France"; and of Barbès, Marx thought him "the scourge of the establishment." In the late 1830s, Barbès wrote a fascinatingly titled pamphlet: *A Few Words to Those Who Sympathize With Workers Without Work*.

32. Some of Marx's portrayals of children's suffering in the "Working Day" chapter (especially Section 3) resemble Ivan's harrowing descriptions in *The Brothers Karamazov*. Dostoevsky has Ivan ask whether the unmitigated suffering of human beings is "due to men's bad qualities or whether it is inherent in their nature?" Ivan believes the latter to be true; he cites, as evidence, numerous newspaper reports of barbarity toward children. Marx knew about the suffering of children—from his own children who'd predeceased him and the children he'd read about in factories. But he would part company with Ivan because he views these pathologies as predominantly societal, not essential.

33. In German, the word for "mole's work"—*maulwurfsarbeit*—is also the term used for clandestine political activity.

34.   Marx had been reading Shakespeare, initially in German translation, since the mid-1830s. As a young man, his future father-in-law, Baron Von Westphalen, introduced the English bard to the young romantic Karl. The Baron, an extremely cultured and polyglot man, was something of an old romantic himself. He devoted a lot of time to Karl, doted on him, and they walked and read Shakespeare together. Shakespeare was one of the Baron's true passions in life and he passed this on to Karl. Eleanor Marx recalled after her father's death how Shakespeare was "the Bible of the house, seldom out of our hands or mouths. By the time I was six I knew scene upon scene of Shakespeare by heart." Her father and mother could recite whole scenes from Shakespeare by heart as well; and on summer Sundays, the whole Marx family would reenact these scenes, picnicking on Hampstead Heath.

35.   In the 1850s, Marx was close to the Chartist movement, on good terms with its leader Ernest Jones. Jones pushed Marx's idea of class struggle and the capital-labor contradiction as a central principle of Chartism. Like Marx, Jones tried to ratchet up the stakes within the working class labor movement, emphasizing the need to move beyond purely defensive union interests, demands resolvable *inside* the capitalist system. The working class didn't just need more pay and fewer hours at work; it needed to conquer political power, to overthrow the bourgeois state. Jones was editor of the *People's Paper*, which Marx read, approved of, and occasionally wrote for.

36.   The League's roots, dating back to the mid-1830s, lay in Blanqui's "Society of the Seasons," and throughout the early 1840s political activity centered in Paris. But the Seasons morphed into another organization called "The Society of the Just," whose activities increasingly lurched toward London, hiding behind the German Workers' Educational Association, founded by the German communist refugee Karl Schapper in 1840.

37.   This is what Marx says there: "The Communists, therefore, are on the one hand, practically, the most advanced and reso-

lute section of the working class parties of every country, that section which pushes forward all others; on the other hand, theoretically they have over the great mass of the proletariat the advantage of clearly understanding the line of march, the conditions, and the ultimate general results of the proletarian movement."

38. See Andy Merrifield, *The Amateur* (London: Verso, 2017).

39. In *To the Finland Station*, Edmund Wilson tells how Lenin refused to listen to the Beethoven he so loved: he feared the wonderful music would touch him, would make him soft, inspire him to drop his steely guard, his rock-hard demeanor. "I know nothing greater than [Beethoven's] *Appassionata*," Wilson quotes Lenin saying. "I'd like to listen to it everyday. It is marvelous superhuman music." "Then," says Wilson, "screwing up his eyes and smiling, Lenin added, rather sadly: 'But I can't listen to music too often. It affects your nerves, makes you want to say stupid nice things and stroke the heads of people. . . . And now you mustn't stroke anyone's head—you might get your hand bitten off. You have to hit them on the head, without any mercy.'"

40. As I write (October 2019), 46,000 members of the United Auto Workers' union (UAW) have been on strike at General Motors (GM) plants across America. The US working class has shown its collective public face at last. Since mid-September, workers have brought factories to a standstill, costing GM so far $113 million in lost profits, haemorrhaging around $25 million a day. Strikers are demanding wage hikes, greater GM share of worker health costs, and the building of more plants for battery-powered vehicles to create jobs.

41. There have been some modest yet significant inroads to unite "gig economy" workers, to create solidarity among them. In recent years, the Independent Workers Union of Great Britain (IWGB) tried to organize bicycle couriers and Uber drivers, and outsourced cleaners and security guards, a workforce hitherto non-unionized and underrepresented. Across the UK, IWGB now has seven branches, leading regional cam-

paigns for better pay, conditions and rights for those "bogusly classified as independent contractors," as if that is some kind of blessing.

42. See "Shoebox Britain: How Shrinking Homes Are Affecting our Health and Happiness," *The Guardian*, October 10, 2018.

43. When *Waiting for Godot* was first performed in Paris in 1952, it coincided, perhaps not by chance, with the publication of Jean-Paul Clébert's *Paris Insolite*, a book about the postwar Parisian poor, about their efforts to stay warm, to eat and drink in the *Zone*, in a no-man's-land of homeless panhandlers and rag-and-bone men, prostitutes and scrap metal dealers. It was war's aftermath; yet another war had commenced. Clébert himself took to the streets, lived with these destitute souls, recounted their tales as one of them. They were Beckett's people, looking and sounding like his *dramatis personae*, right down to their dress sense, their wiles, their visions of who they were, and how they got there. Yet Beckett's brilliance wasn't only to dramatize this zeitgeist; he heard what went on inside these people's heads, too, he voiced their stuttering broken words, their private language, their lack of language. He still voices this lack today, what goes on inside our bedsits and basement flats.

44. The sole concession to modern security has been the installation of three discrete, almost invisible, CCTV cameras around the grave, perched up in nearby trees, with highly sensitive night vision.